ECUMENICAL COUNCILS
OF THE
CATHOLIC CHURCH

ECUMENICAL COUNCILS
OF THE
CATHOLIC CHURCH

An Historical Survey

by

Hubert Jedin

DEUS BOOKS
PAULIST PRESS
(Paulist Fathers)
New York, N. Y.

A Deus Books Edition of the Paulist Press, 1961, by special arrangement with Herder and Herder, Inc., New York, N. Y.

This translation by Ernest Graf, O.S.B., was made from the original version of "Kleine Konziliengeschichte," published by Herder, Freiburg, 1959.

Third Impression published 1960 by
Herder and Herder, Inc.

IMPRIMI POTEST: Placidus Stooper, O.S.B.
Abbas de Buckfast

NIHIL OBSTAT: Adrianus van Vliet, S.T.D.
Censor Deputatus

IMPRIMATUR: E. Morrogh Bernard, *Vic. Gen.*

Westmonasterii, die 31a Octobris, 1959

The Nihil Obstat and Imprimatur are official declarations that a book or pamphlet is free of doctrinal or moral error. No implication is contained therein that those who have granted the Nihil Obstat and Imprimatur agree with the contents, opinions or statements expressed.

© 1960 by Herder KG

Library of Congress
Catalog Card Number: 59-15483

Manufactured in the
United States of America by
Paulist Press, New York, N. Y.

CONTENTS

II
THE PAPAL COUNCILS
OF THE CENTRAL MIDDLE AGES.......... 52

III
THE COUNCIL
ABOVE THE POPE? 84

IV
THE RELIGIOUS DIVISION
AND THE COUNCIL OF TRENT............. 111

8 Contents

EXPLANATION
OF TERMS

According to Canon Law as at present in force [1] an ecumenical council is an assembly of bishops and other specified persons invested with jurisdiction, convoked by the Pope and presided over by him, for the purpose of formulating decisions on questions of the Christian faith or ecclesiastical discipline. These decisions, however, require papal confirmation. The persons entitled to take part in such an assembly are the cardinals (even if they have not received episcopal consecration), the patriarchs, archbishops and bishops, titular bishops included (the latter, however, only if they have been expressly mentioned in the convocation), the abbot primate and the abbots general of the monastic congregations, the superiors general of the exempt Orders and such abbots and prelates as exercise jurisdiction over a district of their own. The right of participation is vested in the person; delegation is permissible but does not entitle the proxy to a plural vote. With the consent of the leaders of the assembly, individual members may make proposals for the conciliar agenda. The ecumenical council wields supreme authority over the Universal Church.

---

[1] C. J. C. Can. 222-29.

Distinct from ecumenical councils are the provincial councils of the bishops of a particular ecclesiastical province, presided over by their metropolitan, and plenary councils which embrace more than one ecclesiastical province and are presided over by a papal legate.[2] Diocesan synods convened by local bishops are not councils in the strict sense of the word because in them the bishop is the sole legislator.

While provincial councils are connected with the ancient ecclesiastical institution of metropolitans, the plenary councils include the bishops of several ecclesiastical provinces, of a whole country, or of a group of territories in which coordination of missionary and pastoral activities seems desirable. Thus the three plenary councils of Baltimore (1852-84), brought about the organization of the pastoral ministry in the United States of America.

Likewise distinct from provincial and plenary councils, as understood by Canon Law, are the meetings of bishops periodically held in many countries, under the presidency of the prelate senior in rank, a cardinal, as the case may be, or by the competent nuncio or apostolic delegate. These meetings deal with the common concerns of the dioceses of the respective country, but unlike the councils they lack legislative power, so that the decisions arrived at do not have force of law for its members. In missionary territories these episcopal conferences may affect the bishops of entire regions, as for instance the conference held at Manila from December 10 to 17, 1958, in which more than a hundred bishops from various countries of the Far-East, from Japan to Indonesia, met under the presidency of Cardinal Agagianian.

In the present work we are not concerned with episcopal conferences or with councils of a lesser rank,

---

2 C. J. C. Can. 281-3.

but deal exclusively with those assemblies, twenty in all, which the Church recognizes as ecumenical. For the first millenium, and even beyond it, the ecumenical character of these assemblies is not decided by the intention of those who convened them, even if they wished them to have that character; in fact, during the whole of this period even papal approval of the decisions does not, from the first, bear the character of a formal confirmation, as was the case with regard to the ecumenical councils of a later period. The recognition of the ecumenical character of the twenty assemblies cannot be traced back to one comprehensive legislative act of the Popes. Their ecumenical character was only established by the theological schools and by actual practice.

The process that led to this acceptance has not as yet been studied in detail, but even now we may say that by the beginning of the sixteenth century the eight ecumenical councils of Christian antiquity were recognized as such. There was some uncertainty about the first Councils of the Lateran and, for obvious reasons, the Council of Basle. In his work *De Concilio*, written during the fifth Lateran Council but published only in 1538, Cardinal Domenico Jacobazzi omitted the first and second Councils of the Lateran, as well as the Council of Basle. Bishop Matthias Ugoni, in his work on the councils, published in 1532, followed the same pattern. At the Council of Trent some of the Spanish and French bishops were unwilling to acknowledge the ecumenical character of the fifth Council of the Lateran. Cardinal Bellarmine was the first to use our present enumeration. For the Roman Collection of the councils [3] the Cardinal drew up a "Warning to the Reader," in respect of the Coun-

---

[3] See *Bibliography*, p. 240.

cil of Basle. It was not printed because the acts of that council were not included in the publication.

Thus historical reality is much more varied than the clear-cut descriptions and definitions of the Church's code of laws would lead one to imagine. In point of fact there are various kinds of councils and to distinguish among them is not always easy even for students of history.

The council of the Apostles and the elders described in the Acts of the Apostles (15:6-29), was subsequently regarded as the prototype of the assemblies of bishops which Christian antiquity designated by the title of synods (from *synodos*—assembly, or even the locality of the assembly). In that first council Paul and Barnabas so successfully championed the freedom of the gentile Christians from the observances of the Mosaic Law, that the compromise proposed by James was accepted and communicated to the Church of **Antioch:** "It is the Holy Spirit's pleasure and ours that no burden should be laid upon you beyond these, which cannot be avoided: you are to abstain from what is sacrificed to idols, from blood-meat and meat which has been strangled, and from fornication." The eighty-five *Apostolic Canons,* believed to have been compiled by Clement of Rome, and handed down to us in Book VIII of the *Apostolic Constitutions,* do not go back to the days of the Apostles; they were probably drawn up as late as the beginning of the fifth century and are based on the canons of earlier councils, chiefly one held at Antioch in the year 341. In the Middle Ages they were regarded as genuine.

It may be questioned whether the earliest known episcopal synods, namely, those held in Asia Minor, in the second half of the second century for the purpose of countering the sect of the Montanists, were conducted after the pattern of the Council of Jerusalem, just as it cannot be shown that they were modeled on the Roman provincial synods. The most obvious explanation is that the bishops of adjoining dioceses would come together in order to take counsel and to devise measures against errors and divisions involving the faith which troubled their respective communities. It was natural that on such occasions the initiative as well as precedence was due to the churches founded by the Apostles; thus in 197 Victor, Bishop of Rome, convoked a synod which took a firm stand against the Eastern practice concerning the date of Easter.

In the third century the holding of episcopal synods was an established custom, partly connected with, and at times ranging beyond, the rising authority of the metropolitans. In the year 256 the Bishop of Carthage, St. Cyprian, convened eighty-seven African bishops for the purpose of obtaining support for his views on the invalidity of heretical Baptism. Early in the fourth century nineteen Bishops and twenty-four priests from every province of the Spanish peninsula met at Elvira where they drew up eighty-one canons on ecclesiastical discipline which have come down to us. Though the competence of these synods was not as yet clearly defined, these assemblies were conscious of acting as witnesses to tradition, but their authority depended on whether their decisions would be accepted by the universal Church. By the beginning of the fourth century episcopal synods were a permanent institution, as is proved by canon 5 of the Council of Nicaea which ordains that two such assemblies must be held every year.

The possibility, as well as the necessity of bringing together the bishops of the whole civilized world, that is, the Graeco-Roman world, only arose after Christianity had secured toleration under Constantine the

Great and had become the predominant religion of the empire. Unity and order in the Church was achieved henceforth also in the interest of the State. As early as the year 314 Constantine convened a synod at Arles which was attended by thirty-three bishops from every part of the Western half of the empire. It dealt with the Donatist dispute which had broken out in Africa, about heretical Baptism and the date of Easter. Ten years later came the first ecumenical synod at Nicaea which was also a council of the empire (see I). However, we must not overlook the fact that a number of these councils were planned as ecumenical councils, but failed to be recognized as such, as for instance Sardica (343) and Seleucia and Rimini (359-60) which met separately, the former for the East, the latter for the West, while on the contrary the Council of Constantinople (381), which was intended only for the eastern half of the empire, eventually obtained ecumenical recognition in the West also, both on account of its dogmatic definitions concerning the divinity of the Holy Ghost and by reason of the authority of the Roman Pontiff.

Side by side with the consolidation of the authority of the metropolitans and the patriarchs went the development of corresponding types of synods, namely, patriarchal synods which used to be convened by the Patriarchs of Alexandria, Antioch and, somewhat later, the Patriarch of Constantinople, and provincial synods which, in the East, were held twice a year for the purpose of examining the appointment and consecration of bishops and settling quarrels. At Carthage plenary councils of the African bishops were held which were not limited to one ecclesiastical province or patriarchate. We can say without exaggeration that the throbbing pulse of the early Church is felt in these synods. Ecumenical councils were the keystone of the whole synodal structure.

A new type of council appeared in the Germanic states, where the rulers exercised paramount influence over the churches of their territories. These councils of the empire or national councils, combined at times with the imperial assemblies of secular magnates but not identical with them, were known as "general synods" or "general councils," because they were not limited to the bishops of an ecclesiastical province but comprised the whole empire; but they were not general councils in the sense which we now attach to that word. It was the bishops' custom, even in mixed assemblies, to discuss ecclesiastical questions separately, although their decisions were sometimes promulgated by the sovereign as laws of the realm, as was done on one occasion during the Carolingian period. All through the early Middle Ages the German kings were used to convening, both in Germany and in Italy, national synods which were often attended by secular princes, without detriment to their ecclesiastical character. Besides these national synods exclusively episcopal synods were also held, for instance those convened by the Archbishop of Mainz, Aribo, at Seligenstadt and Höchst (1223-4). In England the national assemblies were kept separate from the national synods which were presided over by the Archbishop of Canterbury.

If in the Visigothic, Frankish and Germanic national councils, which were convened by the sovereign, there were the beginnings of "secular domination" over the Church, in the councils convened by the Popes, after the Gregorian reform had gained ground, we witness the rise of a reforming papacy fighting for the freedom of the Church. The reform councils of Leo IX and the Roman Lenten synods of his successors prepared the way for those papal general councils of the Middle Ages which came to be recognized as ecumenical (see II).

The paramount position of the papacy in the twelfth century appears from the fact that from this time, and more particularly in the thirteenth century, national councils were presided over by papal legates, as in 1256 at Gran, for Hungary; in 1263 in Paris, for France; in 1287 at Würzburg, for Germany. This type disappears in the fourteenth century, with the rise of the western national states and the weakening of the papacy by the Great Schism. National assemblies of bishops and clergy which were organized without papal aid (they carefully refrained from styling themselves national councils), labored for the most part under anti-papal tendencies, as for instance the national councils of Paris in the years 1395, 1398 and 1406, which concerned themselves with the healing of the schism. This was the time when everything else having failed, an ecumenical council should have finally endeavored to end the schism; however, under the influence of conciliar theory it claimed for itself supreme authority—even over the Pope (see III).

But it was chiefly in the religious divisions of the sixteenth century that national councils, whether only planned or actually held, became a source of constant anxiety for the Popes and a weighty argument for convening an ecumenical council. The German national council which was planned at Speyer in 1524, was never held, but the "assembly of the clergy" at Poissy in 1561, which was combined with a religious *colloquium* and was equivalent to a national council, strengthened Pius IV's resolve to reopen the Council of Trent (see IV).

Through the Tridentine reform a revival was brought about of the provincial councils which had fallen into almost universal desuetude since the fourteenth century. The provincial councils organized by St. Charles Borromeo for the province of Milan were to be the pattern for many others. The "Assemblies of the French Clergy," from the fifteenth to the eighteenth century, were not councils; their chief purpose was to authorize the King to raise taxes, and it was the *assemblée* of 1682 which accepted the four Gallican Articles.

It is often thought that ecumenical councils are those which unite the totality of the episcopate of the inhabited world. But this condition was not even fulfilled at the Vatican Council (see V), and there have been ecumenical councils in which by no means every ecclesiastical province was represented. It must above all be stated that our conception of the ecumenical council has nothing in common with what today is known as "the ecumenical movement"; all that the term implies is that a substantial portion of the episcopate of the world was present at these assemblies and that their decisions were accepted by the universal Church and confirmed by the Pope. In the actual state of theological opinion and according to Canon Law, the latter condition is the decisive one. One modern theologian, Froget, has defined the general or ecumenical council as "a solemn assembly of the bishops of the whole world, convened by the Pope and subject to his authority and guidance, for the purpose of discussing together matters that concern the whole Church and promulgating appropriate legislation." The history of the councils throws light on the road which this institution has traversed from the beginning until it reached its present form.

I
THE EIGHT
ECUMENICAL COUNCILS
OF CHRISTIAN ANTIQUITY

The eight ecumenical councils convened by the Roman, and later on by the Byzantine emperors, which were held in the eastern half of the empire, at Nicaea, Constantinople, Ephesus and Chalcedon, differ so profoundly from all those that came after them and which were called by the Popes, that we are justified in treating them as an historical unit, in spite of the fact that chronologically they overlap into the early Middle Ages and that the first four of them—the "ancient councils" in the strict sense of the word—differ markedly, by reason of their significance, from those that followed.

On account of their authority Pope Gregory the Great compared the first four councils to the four gospels, because they formulated the basic dogmas of the Church—the Trinity and the Incarnation. By comparison with this supremely important task all the other questions discussed in these assemblies were of secondary importance. If we mention some of them our only purpose is to illuminate the close connection of the councils with the contemporary situation of the Church.

The question whether the early councils were convened by the emperors with the previous assent of the Bishop of Rome, or even by his commission, has been the subject of controversy from the time of the reformation. More recently the question was once more vehemently debated between Scheeben, the theologian, and Funk, the Church historian. As far as the facts go, the question may be answered in the negative, but the essential prerogatives of the papacy are not in any way in question. It is equally certain that, as patriarch of the West, and in virtue of a unique precedence, the Popes were represented in these assemblies by legates who were given preferential treatment and who at times presided over the assemblies. Moreover, the Popes' approval of the conciliar decisions was an indispensable requisite for their universal validity.

Constantine the Great had given to the Church her freedom but he had also "tied the Church to the *Imperium* and the *Imperium* to the Church."[1] However, both Church and State were disturbed by a dispute over a question of paramount importance, none other, in fact, than the person of her founder, whom the early Church worshiped as her Lord (*Kyrios*) and set by the side of God, whose Son he had claimed to be. Faithful to the charge laid on her by Christ, the Church administered Baptism in the name of the Father, the Son and the Holy Ghost. How were faith in Christ the Lord, and the Trinitarian formula of Baptism, to be combined with the strict monotheistic faith which the Church had taken over from Judaism?

Toward the end of the second century all the acumen of theological speculation was brought to bear upon this mystery. Greek thought, with the notion of

---

[1] Schwartz, *Uber die Bischofslisten der Synoden von Chalkedon, Nicaea und Konstantinopel* (1937).

the Logos and the creator of the world (the demiurge), the highest of a whole scale of intermediary beings between God and man, seemed to point to a way by which the human mind might extricate itself from what looked like a dilemma. The teaching of more than one theologian of the third century followed Greek thought, even though they may not have gone as far as Sabellius who described the three Persons, Father, Son and Holy Ghost, as so many manifestations of the one God (*modalismus*), or taught "subordinationism," that is, assigned to the Son a position inferior to that of the Father. But this notion was taken over by Arius, a priest of Alexandria, from his teacher, Lucian of Antioch, and carried still further. In his opinion the Logos was "a creature of the Father," lacking the attribute of eternity: "There was a time when he was not."

Arius was not an isolated thinker. As a religious personality of considerable charm and an able writer he recruited many followers, so that he found himself at the head of a community of his own. On account of his teaching he was excommunicated by his bishop, Alexander, in a great synod (318), but by that time Arianism had been consolidated. An attempt at mediation by a trusted adviser of the emperor, Bishop Hosius of Cordova, proved fruitless. The conflict raised a great storm throughout the East.

The "Great and Holy Synod of the 318 Fathers at Nicaea" (325)

There were other causes of unrest in the Church at this time, as for instance the controversy over the date of Easter. Constantine accordingly invited the bishops of the empire to Nicaea in Bithynia, and he issued orders that, like the high officials of the State, they should have the use of the transport provided by the imperial post. The number of the bishops who obeyed the summons—usually given as 318—is due to a Biblical reminiscence, the 318 servants of Abraham (Gen. 14:14); in reality it is not likely that their number greatly exceeded the 220 whose names we know. Eusebius of Caesarea, the "father of Church history," mentioned 250 names, and stressed the fact that they came from every corner of the earth. The council, he wrote, included prelates from "Syria and Cilicia, Phoenicia, Arabia, Palestine, Egypt, Thebes, Libya, and strangers from Mesopotamia. One bishop came even from as far as Persia to take part in the synod, nor was Scythia unrepresented, while Pontus and Galatia, Cappadocia and Asia, Phrygia and Pamphylia sent their most distinguished bishops. Men came from Thrace and Macedonia, Achaia and Epirus, and from even more distant countries, and one of the many members of the assembly was that illustrious man, Hosius, who had come from Spain. But on account of his advanced years, Sylvester, the bishop of the imperial city (Rome), was not present; in his place he sent priests to represent him." From the West only five priests attended.

The council sat from May 20 to July 25, 325, in one of the halls of the imperial summer residence at Nicaea. The Emperor made a personal appearance and delivered a Latin address in which he urged the assembly to restore peace. He did not intervene in the discussions but, according to Eusebius, "left the direction of the council to its leaders." Who these were is uncertain because we have no official records of this council, nor of those that followed it.

Not a few among the bishops "bore the stigmata of our Lord Jesus Christ in their body," because they had been steadfast witnesses to the faith during the previous persecutions. Their number included Paul of Neocaesarea, on the Euphrates, whose hands were paralyzed, because his sinews had been burned with red-hot irons. And there was Paphnutius, an Egyptian, who had lost an eye during the persecution of Maximinus.

Arius defended his teaching in person. The most influential of his seventeen partisans was the court-bishop Eusebius of Nicomedia. By means of lengthy discussions, many contests and careful considerations, the orthodox opposition party, led by Bishop Marcellus of Ancyra (the modern Ankara), Bishop Eustathius of Antioch and the Alexandrian deacon Athanasius, obtained the upper hand and on the basis of the baptismal symbol of the church of Caesarea, submitted by its Bishop, Eusebius, formulated the Nicene Creed the unequivocal terms of which preclude any kind of subordination of the Son to the Father. The Son is said to be "of the Father's substance, God of God, Light of light, true God of true God, begotten, not made, of the same substance as the Father" (*homoousios*). In an appendix the most important theses of Arius were expressly condemned. The Creed was approved by the council on June 19, 325. Only two bishops refused to sign it. Together with Arius they were excommunicated and banished. The Emperor promulgated the Creed as a law of the empire.

Minor problems occupied the council for yet another month. As for the computation of the date of Easter, there was general agreement that the feast should be observed on the first Sunday following the first full moon after the spring equinox—a custom that obtains to this day. The Bishop of that seat of learning, Alexandria, was commissioned to compute and announce the date each year. To this decision the Emperor also gave force of law for the whole empire. Bishop Meletius of Lycopolis, as a rigorist, was dissatisfied with the mild treatment which the Bishop of Alexandria meted out to those who had failed to stand the test during the persecution of Diocletian.

He was told not to interfere with the latter's administration. In twenty brief decisions the council defined its attitude in regard to some minor controversies and abuses, thereby laying down directives for the life of the Church (hence the word canon = rule, standard). These canons, like those of the later councils, illuminate the situation of the Church at the time of their formulation. It was necessary to advance from the situation created by the era of persecution. Canon 11 decreed, that those who had apostatized during the persecution of Licinius were to be readmitted to full communion after a penance of twelve years, divided into three stages. The numerous converts to Christianity, after the Church had secured her freedom, included opportunists and place-hunters. Against these, canon 2 reaffirmed the existing law, which prescribed that neophytes could only be raised to the priesthood, or the episcopate, after a prolonged period of probation. Other canons dealt with the constitution and the liturgy of the Church. Canon 4 ordained that episcopal consecration must be conferred by at least three bishops. Canon 6 subordinated the metropolitan and other bishops of Egypt, Libya and the Thebaid to the Bishop of Alexandria who accordingly occupied a patriarchal position similar to that of the Bishop of Rome. Canon 20 decreed that on Sundays and during the whole of Eastertide, Christians should pray standing. Canon 17 was directed against usury, and was renewed again and again by later councils.

The Greek Church historian, Socrates, relates that the council of Nicaea wished to enforce the law of celibacy for bishops and priests, but that it refrained from doing so as a result of the intervention of Bishop Paphnutius, a confessor of the faith, who warned the assembly against laying too heavy a burden on the clergy. The story is credible enough;

what is certain is that the council approved the Eastern custom which forbids unmarried priests to marry after ordination but allows those already married to continue their married life. Canon 3 allowed a cleric to live under the same roof with his mother, sister or aunt, or with such persons who would cause no scandal.

At the conclusion of the conciliar discussions Constantine, who was then celebrating the twentieth anniversary of his accession to power, entertained the bishops at so splendid a banquet that Eusebius concludes his description of it with the remark that "one might have thought the whole thing was a dream, not solid reality." The full splendor of the imperial majesty and a restored empire fell upon this first ecumenical council of the Church, so recently risen from persecution. But the longed-for peace was not achieved, in fact the council proved to be the starting point of violent conflicts which were to last over half a century.

Controversy Over the Council of Nicaea

Not many years after the council the middle party led by Eusebius of Nicomedia, which favored Arius, but had been defeated at Nicaea, succeeded in gaining influence over Constantine. A relentless campaign was started against the head of the orthodox party, Athanasius, who in the meantime had been raised to the see of Alexandria. In 335 Athanasius was banished to Trier. Arius' rehabilitation was only prevented by his death in 336. A new general council at Sardica, the modern Sofia, in 342, not only failed to restore unity in the Church but actually led to a fresh conflict. While the western bishops declared the deposition of Athanasius to be unjust, and renewed their approval of the Nicene Creed, the eastern prelates, who met separately, condemned Athanasius as well as Pope Julius I with whom he had found refuge. They drew up a new formula which evaded the Nicene term "consubstantial" (*homoousios*). Many compromise formulas were invented, such as "the Son is like to the Father," "in all respects like to the Father," is "of a nature like that of the Father."

The opponents of the Nicene Creed persuaded the pro-Arian Emperor Constantine to convoke another general synod. This assembly met in the year 359, at Rimini for the West and at Seleucia for the East, but no reconciliation was effected. The bishops gathered at Rimini, roughly four hundred, reaffirmed the Nicene Creed while those at Seleucia failed to agree among themselves. Constantine threatened with banishment those bishops who refused to put their signature to a formula evolved at Nice (Niké)—"The Father and the Son are alike in substance, according to Scripture" — (*Nicenum* instead of *Nicaenum*). Though Pope Liberius and St. Hilary of Poitiers refused to sign, St. Jerome's saying of a later date: "The whole world groaned and marveled to find itself Arian," was not without a grain of truth.

There was no change until Constantine's death (361). His successor, Julian the Apostate, who abhorred Christianity, entertained the hope that his order for the return from exile of the bishops of both parties would lead to its disruption and destruction from within, but this expectation was not fulfilled. The Emperor Valens, who had Arian leanings, was also unable to arrest the splitting up and the decline of Arianism and of Semi-Arianism which included the many varieties of moderate Arianism. The policy of pacification of the Catholic-minded Emperor Gratian (375-83) and Pope Damasus I (366-84) prevailed in the East also, and all the more rapidly as the so-called "Young Nicenes," that is the three great Cappadocians: Basil, Gregory Nazianzen and Gregory of Nyssa, had cleared away the theological misconceptions which prevented a proper understanding of the Nicene formula, summed up by them in the words: "one essence, three persons." One can understand that at first the strict "Old Nicenes" at Alexandria and in the West should have viewed this solution with some mistrust. At Antioch, where a schism had broken out, they supported the "Old Nicene" Paulinus against the "Young Nicene" Meletius. The Emperor Theodosius I resolved to remove the remaining tensions and to seal the peace by means of yet another imperial council which would insert the keystone into the Trinitarian Creed, by defining the divinity of the Holy Ghost. Logically enough, from their standpoint, both Arians and Semi-Arians had declared the Holy Ghost to be a creature of the Son. St. Athanasius had countered them in two synods held at Alexandria in 362 and 363. Several Roman synods had likewise condemned "the opponents of the Holy Ghost" (Pneumatomachi). Macedonius, Bishop of Constantinople, was one of their number and for that reason they were sometimes called Macedonians.

The Ecumenical Council of Constantinople (381)

The general synod convened by the Emperor Theodosius at Constantinople, which opened in May, 381, was only attended by the eastern bishops. This fact would account by itself alone for the small number of its members—about 150—which was less than at Nicaea. Pope Damasus was neither personally present, nor was he represented. The western bishops had met at Aquileia in the spring of the same year. Our information about the discussions is even scantier than about those of Nicaea. The assembly was at first presided over by Meletius, Patriarch of Antioch, who enjoyed the favor of Theodosius. There were also

present St. Gregory Nazianzen, whose promotion to
the see of Constantinople (in the place of Macedonius) was confirmed by the council, and St. Cyril of
Jerusalem, whose *catecheses mystagogicae* are reckoned among the most precious gems of early Christian
literature. Every effort to convince the thirty-six
Macedonians of their error was in vain and they left
the city. After the death of Meletius, Gregory Nazianzen presided for a time but withdrew when his efforts
to heal the Antiochene schism by the elevation of
Paulinus to the vacant see, met with strong opposition within the synod and a priest named Flavian, a
friend of the deceased patriarch, was chosen to succeed him. However, as Gregory Nazianzen puts it in
his report, "a sharper wind from the West blew into
the synod" with the arrival of the Egyptian bishops
who came in obedience to a new and pressing invitation from the Emperor. For the sake of peace
Gregory resigned the see of Constantinople and delivered his famous farewell oration. From that moment his successor Nectarius presided over the council
up to its conclusion in July of the same year.

The first of its four authentic canons proclaimed
anew the faith of Nicaea and summarily condemned
the various tendencies of the Arians, the Semi-Arians,
or pneumatomachi, who were all lumped together, as
well as the Sabellians. In keeping with the new status
of Constantinople as the residence of the Emperor,
canon 3 granted to the bishop of the capital precedence over all other patriarchs of the Eastern Church,
but after the Bishop of Rome. Canons 5, 6 and 7,
which Greek tradition ascribes to the ecumenical council of Constantinople, do not belong to that assembly,
but to a synod of the year 382, also held at Constantinople, which forwarded the decrees of the council of
the previous year to the bishops of the West. However, it did not succeed in obtaining recognition for

the canons, on account of Rome's refusal to accept
canon 3, but the Creed formulated after the departure of the Macedonians was approved by the West.

The Creed, usually described as *Symbolum Nicaeno-
Constantinopolitanum,* and traced back to these two
councils, was in reality a baptismal profession of
faith which Epiphanius, Bishop of Constantia in the
island of Cyprus, had advocated in his book entitled
Ancoratus. The formula seems to have originated in
Jerusalem. Its first part is identical with the Nicene
Creed, but it contains an additional clause affirming
the divinity of the Holy Ghost, "Lord and life-giver,
who proceeds from the Father, who is worshiped and
glorified in the same way as the Father, who has spoken by the prophets."

After the recognition of the second Council of Constantinople of the year 381 as ecumenical, this Creed
became the authentic profession of faith of the Greek
Church. It was likewise accepted by the Western
Church, and is used to this day in the Roman Mass,
though with the addition of a short clause, the insertion of which was fraught with grave consequences.
The fact was that the Greeks understood the formula
"who proceeds from the Father" to mean "from the
Father through the Son," while the West interpreted
it as meaning "from the Father and the Son." The
additional clause *filioque,* first heard of in Spain, also
found a place in the rhythmic Creed *Quicumque vult
salvus esse*—erroneously ascribed to St. Athanasius.
The clause became a cause of discord between East
and West, for the Greeks refused to regard it as explanatory and considered it a falsification of the hal-
lowed text.

Two Schools — Two Views of Christ

It was only natural that after the precise, dogmatic
definitions of the doctrine of the Trinity, by the first

two ecumenical councils, theologians would try to explore still further the mystery of Christ's person. Yet when they entered on this task they did not follow the dictates of logic, but were moved by an opposition of long-standing between two theological schools, an opposition rendered still more acute by a rivalry which was in part political and in part ecclesiastical.

The Alexandrian catechetical school, which revered Clement of Alexandria and Origen, the greatest theologian of the Greek Church, as its heads, applied the allegorical method to the explanation of Scripture. Its thought was influenced by Plato: its strong point was theological speculation. Athanasius and the three Cappadocians had been included among its members, and at the opening of the fifth century, its greatest theologian was St. Cyril, Patriarch of Alexandria since the year 412. Anxious to stress the closeness of the union of divinity and humanity in the person of Jesus Christ, Cyril spoke of "the one nature of the incarnate Logos," and illustrated the statement by means of a striking comparison: "the divine nature," he said, "permeates the human nature as fire permeates red-hot coals or a burning log." He failed to perceive that expressions and comparisons such as these could betray those who heard them into extenuating the human nature of Christ, and into conceiving the union of the two natures as a fusion of them (syncrasis).

On the other hand the Antiochene school, the founder of which is thought to have been Lucian of Antioch (or Samosata) was noted for a careful and sober exegesis, taking account of both grammar and history. More Aristotelian than Platonic, it was not free from rationalism. In the fourth century, Diodorus of Tharsus was its most eminent and greatly honored head (d. before 394). As a conscientious exponent of Scripture, Diodorus insisted with so much earnestness on the fact that Christ was man that he came close to undermining the substantial union with the Godhead, which as a matter of fact he acknowledged, and to reducing it to no more than a moral union. Of this tendency there was scarcely a trace in his illustrious pupil, John Chrysostom, who succeeded Nectarius as Bishop of Constantinople in 398. It was more noticeable in that influential exegete, Theodore of Mopsuestia (d. 428); above all, it was sharply accentuated in the thinking of the latter's pupil, Nestorius, who became Bishop of Constantinople in the year of his master's death. The divergence of the conceptions is clearly seen in the comparison by which the Antiochenes were wont to illustrate the union of the divine and the human nature in Christ: "the Logos dwells in the man Jesus as in a temple," they said.

St. Cyril was Patriarch of Alexandria, Nestorius of Constantinople. The tension arising from the divergence of the theological schools was further sharpened by the rivalry between the two episcopal sees. As the imperial residence on the Bosphorus, Constantinople overshadowed and eventually surpassed Alexandria, hitherto so highly esteemed as a seat of learning and as a bulwark of orthodoxy. St. John Chrysostom (d. 407), had had to suffer in his day from the jealousy of the Patriarch of Alexandria, Theophilus, a man filled with ambition and lust for power. Cyril was Theophilus' nephew as well as his successor, hence it was to be expected that he would make a strong stand against Nestorius' dangerous opinions concerning the person of Christ.

Cyril Against Nestorius

Nestorius was a powerful orator. Faithful to the theological school of Antioch, he objected in his sermons to the title of "Theotókos"—"Mother of God," bestowed on the Mother of Jesus Christ. In his opin-

ion, Mary could only be styled "Christotókos"—
"Christ's mother," for she had given birth to the man
Jesus, in whom God dwelt "as in a temple." But the
faithful were not prepared to give up an encomium
with which they were accustomed to honor the Mother
of God. More than ever Cyril was on the alert. In
429, in his customary Easter-letter to the bishops of
Egypt, and in a circular letter addressed to the most
faithful among his adherents, the monks, of whom
there were many thousands, Cyril reprobated the
teaching of Nestorius and at the same time requested
Pope Celestine I (422-32) to make a pronouncement
on the subject. In a Roman synod in 430, Celestine
expressed his agreement with Cyril's views, where-
upon the latter summoned Nestorius to recant, and at
the same time sent him a list of twelve errors which
he must abjure. The first of these anathematisms, as
they were called, stated: "If anyone refuses to acknowledge that the Emmanuel is true God, and the
Blessed Virgin the Mother of God, let him be anathema." The third anathematism censured an expression
which was current among the Antiochenes, namely, the
conjunction (*synapheia*) of godhead and manhood in
the incarnate Logos. Against it Cyril described the
two natures by a term which was liable to be mis-
understood—namely, "hypostasis" in the sense of
"substance."

Thus in the contest for Mary's title of "Mother of
God," the long-standing opposition between the theological schools of Alexandria and Antioch became
more pronounced. The Patriarch of Antioch, John,
sided with Nestorius on principle, while warning him
at the same time against disturbing the peace of the
Church, since the term Theotókos was susceptible of
an orthodox interpretation. Nestorius remained ob-
durate. Attributed to him are twelve counter anathematisms whose genuineness is argued. The first of

these rejected the term Theotókos, for God merely dwelt in the human nature assumed by him in the womb of the Virgin, but it was at his instigation, in a circular letter dated November 19, 430, and addressed to all the metropolitans of East and West, that the Emperor Theodosius II, acting likewise in the name of Valentinian III, for the West, convoked an ecumenical council which was to assemble at Ephesus by the feast of Pentecost, 431. Ephesus possessed a large church dedicated to the Blessed Virgin Mary, the remains of which have been studied by archaeologists in recent years. This church was to be the seat of the council. We are in a better position to follow up the dramatic course of this assembly than that of previous councils for we possess its acts and a great many letters.

The Title Theotokos and the
Council of Ephesus (431)

In a personal letter the Emperor invited the greatest theologian of the Western Church, Aurelius Augustinus, to come to Ephesus. However, Augustine died in his episcopal city of Hippo, besieged at the time by the Vandals, before the information reached him. Cyril of Alexandria became the dominant personality of the assembly and it was he who opened it, on June 22, 431. In so doing he was also acting as representative of the Pope. The opening had been postponed for sixteen days, but even then the Antiochenes and their Patriarch had not arrived. Although residing at Ephesus, Nestorius refused to attend, in spite of three summonses. Popular feeling in the city was hostile to him, so much so in fact that for the sake of his personal safety, he asked to be protected by soldiers of the imperial bodyguard. His request was granted.

In the course of the opening session a doctrinal exposition, drawn up by Cyril, of the hypostatic union of the two natures in Christ, was read and approved. This was followed by the reading of relevant passages from the writings of the Fathers of the Church, such as bore witness to the ancient faith, and by way of contrast, twenty extracts from the writings of Nestorius were also read. This done, sentence was pronounced against Nestorius, without any doubt, somewhat over-hastily: "Our Lord Jesus Christ, who has been blasphemed by him (Nestorius) has decreed, through this holy synod, that the same Nestorius be deprived of all episcopal dignity and barred from every assembly of bishops." The sentence was signed by all the 198 bishops who had taken part in the session. Meanwhile darkness had fallen, so the bishops were escorted to their lodgings by a jubilant people carrying lighted torches.

The Emperor's conciliar commissary, Candidian, had protested against the opening of the council in the absence of the Antiochenes. His report, and that of Nestorius, were despatched to the Emperor, but so was that of the council. It was at this moment (June 26 or 27), that the forty-three Antiochene bishops appeared on the scene. They constituted themselves into an opposition-council and excommunicated both Cyril and the local Bishop of Ephesus, Memnon, who next to, and together with, Cyril, was held responsible for what had taken place. They also justified their conduct before the Emperor. Theodosius roundly declared null and void all that had been done up to this time. The Antiochenes were jubilant—too soon.

The second session was held at the residence of Bishop Memnon, when the council welcomed the three legates sent by the Pope, two of them bishops, the third a simple priest. In its fourth session, on July 16, the council declared the sentences pronounced by the Antiochene *conciliabulum* to be null and void. In its fifth session, on July 17, it pronounced a sentence of excommunication against Patriarch John and his adherents. Finally, in the seventh and last session, probably on July 31, held once more in the church of the Blessed Virgin Mary, the council gave its approval to six canons directed against Nestorius and his party. A circular letter informed the absent bishops of all that had been done.

The Nestorians had contrived to intercept all the letters addressed to the Emperor by Cyril and by the conciliar majority. However, a messenger disguised as a beggar, successfully smuggled into Constantinople a letter of Cyril's addressed to the monks of the city, all of them hostile to Nestorius. The letter—no longer extant—had been hidden in a hollow cane. Thereupon crowds of monks made their way to the imperial palace; but all they discovered was that Theodosius confirmed the deposition of Nestorius as well as that of Cyril and Memnon, his opponents, who were both thrown into prison. A new conciliar commissary of a higher rank, the treasurer John, was despatched to Ephesus. Everything was now in the balance, but there was no reason to think that the cause of the Antiochenes was lost. Once more they accused Cyril of having misled the majority bishops and of having roused the populace. Their own doctrine they sought to support by means of a new creed. Thereupon the Emperor summoned eight representatives drawn from each party into his presence, to hear their reports. A change now came over him. After a while, the Emperor refused to receive the Antiochene deputies and decisively disavowed Nestorius: "No one must mention that man to me!" he declared. Nestorius was first banished to a monastery in the neighborhood of Antioch and finally to Upper Egypt. To this day opinions are divided as to how far he was a heretic in the strict sense of the word, and to what extent his fate was due to misunderstandings.

The members of the synod were granted leave to return to their respective dioceses—Cyril included. The patriarch, according to Ostrogorsky, "had won a splendid victory both in the theological and in the ecclesiastical and political sphere." On his part, to commemorate the council, Pope Sixtus III (432-40), adorned the triumphal arch of the basilica of Santa Maria Maggiore, recently restored by him, with mosaics glorifying the Blessed Virgin Mary which exist to this day.

The Robber Council (Latrocinium) of Ephesus

Nestorius had been condemned by the Council of Ephesus, but neither the Antiochene school, nor Patriarch John of Antioch and his adherents, shared his fate, so long as they did not obstinately hold on to him. However, sympathizers with Nestorius maintained their ground in the schools of Edessa and Nisibis and in 498 they created a patriarchate of their own at Seleucia—Ctesiphon. From there, during the following centuries, missionaries carried their teaching as far as China and India.

With the moderate Antiochenes Cyril came to terms in 433, when he accepted a profession of faith drawn up by them. It was a compromise but it contained the expression Theotókos. However, before long the germ of an error which was latent even in the Alexandrian view of the person of Christ, sprouted into a fresh heresy, which could only be warded off by yet another council.

Eutyches was the archimandrite (superior) of a monastery in Constantinople and a keen opponent of Nestorius. But he maintained that after the divine nature had been united to the human in the person of Christ, his human nature was merged in the divine, so that from that moment there could only be question of one nature, the divine. Monophysitism, as the heresy was accordingly called, diminished the humanity of our Lord, though his human nature is an essential condition of our redemption. A synod convened at Constantinople by Patriarch Flavian, in 448, condemned Eutyches. However, as was to be expected, the latter had the support of Dioscorus, Patriarch of Alexandria, and Cyril's successor. Dioscorus shared Cyril's enthusiasm for the Alexandrian Christology, but differed from him by reason of his ambition and brutality. At his instigation the Emperor Theodosius II convoked a general council which was to meet once again at Ephesus. In consequence of strong pressure by the military and the monks who had been drafted into the city, Eutyches was rehabilitated. The legates of Pope Leo I were denied the right of presiding and the reading of the Pope's explanatory letter to Patriarch Flavian was likewise forbidden. Leo I described the synod as a "Robbers' Synod"—*latrocinium*. Protests against its decisions came from every quarter. As early as October 13, 449, Pope Leo, in his own name and that of the western bishops, requested the Emperor to convoke a fresh council to be held in Italy. Though twice repeated the request remained unanswered. However, Marcian, who succeeded Theodosius II, assented to the demand. On May 17, 451, he convoked a new council which was to meet, not in Italy but at Nicaea. However, shortly before the opening, the assembly was transferred to Chalcedon, on the Bosphorus, a locality which commended itself on account of its proximity to the capital. The fourth ecumenical council of Chalcedon, though once again convoked by the Emperor, was in fact the work of Leo I on whom history has conferred the title of "the Great." About this assembly we possess abundant sources of information (official protocols, lists of bishops present, letters) so that we are better informed about its course than about that of all the other councils of Christian antiquity.

The Faith of Chalcedon (451)

As regards numbers the Council of Chalcedon surpassed all the earlier councils and most of those that followed, up to the Vatican Council. The number of bishops present at it is usually given as 600; in reality it was a good deal smaller. Numerically the West was only feebly represented, namely by five papal legates three bishops and two priests—who, in accordance with Pope Leo's demand, presided over the synod while the management of conciliar business was in the hands of imperial commissaries appointed for the purpose. There were likewise present two African bishops who had fled from the Vandals. In the very first session held on October 8, 451, in the church of St. Euphemia, Dioscorus, the originator of the Robber Council of Ephesus, was confronted with his accusers, when his deeds of violence were brought to light. In the third session, on October 13, a sentence of deposition was pronounced against him, while mercy was shown to his adherents. In the previous session, the second, the Nicene profession of faith and an *Epistola dogmatica* of Leo the Great on the two natures in Christ, had been read. "This is the faith of the Fathers," the bishops exclaimed, "this is the faith of the Apostles. This is the faith of all of us. Peter has spoken through Leo."

However, certain objections to the formulations of the doctrine of the two natures which had arisen in the minds of the bishops of Palestine and Illyria, had still to be disposed of. The representatives of the Pope objected to a new formulation of the faith since the whole subject had been made abundantly clear. For all that, in the fifth session held on October 22, the council submitted a profession of faith drawn up by twenty-three bishops, the contents of which kept close to the Pope's *Epistola dogmatica*. In the sixth session, at which the Emperor and the Empress assisted, this formula was promulgated and signed by all the bishops. The text is as follows: "We all teach with one voice . . . one and the same Christ, Son, Lord, Only-Begotten, perfect God and perfect man . . . in [not of] two natures, without confusion, without change [against the Monophysites], without separation, without division [against the Nestorians], both natures being united in one person and one hypostasis."

In this sixth session, in which Marcian and his energetic wife, Pulcheria, were accorded the honorary presidency, the council undoubtedly reached its climax. The Fathers regarded it as concluded, but the Emperor was anxious for a settlement of a few questions of discipline and persons, such as the full reinstatement of Theodoret of Cyrus and that of Ibas of Edessa, two leading figures of the school of Antioch. The last of the twenty-eight canons formulated in the sixteenth session, held on October 31, was opposed by the papal legates and in the final session on November 1, they lodged a formal protest against it. This canon was to the effect that the see of the new Rome (Constantinople) should have the same prerogatives as that of the old Rome and should rank second after that see. Though requested by both Emperor and council, Leo the Great refused to confirm this canon which went counter to the doctrine of papal primacy which this Pope understood so clearly and asserted so resolutely.

Canon 6 of the council, which forbade so-called absolute ordinations, that is, ordinations conferred for

no definite ecclesiastical office, as well as canons 3, 4
and 20, which placed monks under the jurisdiction of
the bishops, were sometimes appealed to in the course
of the Tridentine discussions of reform.

The Aftermath of Monophysitism

Chalcedon kept to a middle course between the erroneous views about Christ's person of Nestorius and
those of the Monophysites. It was also a meeting of
East and West, Pope and Emperor and as Grillmaier
put it, "the result of the severe contest of competing
forces, imperial power-politics, rivalry between patriarchs, separate national interests, monkish enthusiasm." However, Monophysitism had struck such deep
roots in Egypt and the adjacent territories that the
faith of Chalcedon was not able to suppress it, were it
only by reason of its having allied itself with the
separatist policy of provinces remote from the center
of the empire. Thus it came about that bloody riots
occurred in Alexandria. A Monophysite became Patriarch and many episcopal sees were occupied by
Monophysites. For more than a century the Byzantine
emperors made desperate efforts to master this latent
and open resistance. At one time one of them drew
up a vague formula of reunion, the Henoticon (482),
and even put up with a breach with Rome—the Schism
of Acacius (484-519). The Emperor Justinian (527-
65), the restorer of the empire, whose wife Theodora
was secretly devoted to Monophysitism, had promoted
the election to the see of Rome of Vigilius who had
represented the Pope at Constantinople and who appeared to be possessed of an accommodating character. With his help the Emperor hoped to overcome
the resistance of the West to any kind of bargain
with the Monophysites. However, in the end Vigilius
professed his adherence to the faith of Chalcedon.

At this stage one of the Emperor's advisers conceived a plan for meeting the Monophysites indirectly, perhaps even conciliating them, by striking at the heads of the Antiochene school. Justinian accordingly published an edict condemning, firstly, the person and writings of Theodore of Mopsuestia; secondly, the writings of Theodoret of Cyrus (d. *c.* 460) against Cyril of Alexandria and the Nicene Creed; thirdly, a letter of Ibas of Edessa in which the latter defended Theodore against Cyril. Here we have the so-called "Three Chapters." The question was to be dealt with by a general council which Justinian convoked at the beginning of 553, with the agreement of Pope Vigilius. The assembly was to meet at Constantinople.

Vigilius was hard pressed. The Emperor had compelled him to come to Constantinople, for after the overthrow of the Kingdom of the Ostrogoths, Italy had come under the authority of the Romans of the east. The Pope was treated as a prisoner, but he succeeded in escaping to Chalcedon. From his place of refuge (the church in which the Council of Chalcedon had been held) he withdrew his promise to appear in person at a council in which he feared the Greeks would outvote all the other bishops. The council, the second of Constantinople, was opened by Patriarch Eutychius, on May 5, 553, in the *secretarium* (sacristy) of the cathedral, in the presence of 150 bishops, but without the Pope and in spite of his protests. One hundred and sixty bishops appended their signature to the acts of the eighth session, the final one, on June 2, 553. In its fifth and sixth sessions held on May 19 and 26, the council condemned the "Three Chapters," in spite of the fact that in a declaration dated May 14, also signed by sixteen bishops, most of them from the West, Vigilius had refused to condemn the person of Theodore and the two other "Chapters." Only at a later date, namely on December 8, 553, and again on February 23, 554, and after he had fully explained the motives of his action, did Vigilius give his assent to the condemnation of all "Three Chapters," thereby paving the way for the recognition of the assembly as an ecumenical council. He had convinced himself that the faith of Chalcedon was not impaired by this act. However, the ecclesiastical provinces of Milan and Aquileia refused for a long time to recognize the council, and the metropolitan of Aquileia, who in the meantime had assumed the title of Patriarch, only resumed communion with Rome in 607.

A fresh attempt to bring the Monophysites back to the Church of the empire was made some time after the council by Patriarch Sergius of Constantinople (610-38). Starting from the moral unity of the theandric operations of Jesus Christ, he assumed that there was only one natural theandric energy and one theandric will in him. A group of moderate Monophysites, the Severians (after Severus of Antioch) allowed themselves to be persuaded, but the adherents of the Council of Chalcedon, above all the monk Sophronius who in 634 had become Patriarch of Jerusalem, offered strong opposition to a formula which had all the air of a questionable compromise. From Pope Honorius I (625-38), who had but a slender grasp of this subtle question, Sergius successfully extracted an approval couched in general terms, but the consequence was that adoption of Monotheletism was prescribed by an imperial law (*Ekthesis*) promulgated in the year 638. However, in a synod held at the Lateran in 649, Pope Martin I (649-55) pronounced against the doctrine and in favor of "two natural wills and modes of operation in Christ. For this he was accused of high treason and banished to the Crimea where he succumbed to the ill-treatment to which he was subjected.

An unequivocal return to the line laid down at

Chalcedon was only made by Constantine III (668-85) at a time when the Byzantine Empire was hard pressed in the North and in the East by the Avars and the Arabs. With the agreement of Pope Agatho (678-81), the Emperor summoned a council to Constantinople. The eight representatives of the Pope were the bearers of a synodal letter in which the patriarchal synod of Rome explained the orthodox doctrine.

The sixth ecumenical council, the third to be held at Constantinople, lasted from November 7, 680 to September 16, 681. The sessions were held in a domed hall of the imperial palace (*trullus*, hence the name *Concilium in Trullo*) and under the presidency of the papal legates. Although those strongholds of Monophysitism, the Patriarchates of Alexandria and Jerusalem, had in the meantime fallen into the hands of the Arabs, and were scarcely represented, the number of those present in the assembly rose to 174. The Emperor Constantine assisted in person at the first eleven sessions. After a thorough examination of the question, and when the weakness of the ostensible proofs furnished by the spokesman of the Monotheletists, Macarius of Alexandria, had been demonstrated, the authors and promoters of Monotheletism were condemned in the thirteenth session, March 28, 681. In the sixteenth session, which was also the last, and at which the Emperor assisted once more, an appropriate profession of faith was agreed to. It declared that the doctrine of two natural wills and two operations in Christ was in conformity with the teaching of the five previous councils. In the acclamations at the conclusion of the session, Constantine was hailed as a new Marcian and a new Justinian.

The Question of Honorius

The list of the men condemned by the sixth ecumenical council for favoring Monothelitism included

the name of Pope Honorius I. The "Question of
Honorius," which was to raise so much dust at the
Vatican Council, comes to this: Was Honorius condemned because he maintained a false doctrine, hence
as a heretic, or was he sentenced solely on account of
carelessness and remissness in relation to this dogmatic problem? The question was answered by Pope
Leo II (682-3) who, while approving the decisions
of the council, restricted the terms of the sentence
against his predecessor so that they were equivalent
to a blame for remissness in repressing heresy.

The fifth and sixth ecumenical councils drew up no
disciplinary canons. The gap was filled by another
synod likewise at Constantinople, in the year 692,
which promulgated 102 canons, almost exclusively
concerned with conditions in the eastern Church,
while western claims (such as the Roman primacy),
and western customs (for example, with regard to fast-
ing) were ignored. Pope Sergius (687-701) refused
to approve these canons although himself of eastern
origin, being a Syrian by birth. This council is regarded by the Greek Church as ecumenical.

The Rise of New Peoples

While the eastern Church, during the years immediately following the Council of Chalcedon, was ex-
pending most of its energy in a contest over subtle
distinctions in Christology, the world underwent a
change. In the course of the invasion of the Bar-
barians, Germanic tribes had founded a new kingdom
on what had been territories of the western empire.
The kingdoms of the Vandals and the Ostrogoths were
of short duration, those of the Visigoths and the Lombards lasted longer, but that of the Franks contained
the seeds of future greatness. In the East the assault
by the Arabs had begun. In a victorious forward
march, which nothing seemed able to check, they had

made themselves masters of Egypt, Syria, Persia, and
Northern Africa. In this way they had forged the iron
ring with which Islam encircled the Christian West
and cut it off from the rest of the world for eight
hundred years. The entry into history of the Germanic and Arabic peoples was not without influence
on the convocation and structure of future councils.
For a time the national churches of the Visigoths and
the Lombards retained their original Roman charac-
teristics, and the bishops contrived to hold their
synods. But before long new types came into being,
such as the national synods convoked by the Mero-
vingian Kings, for instance, that of Orleans in 511,
and later on the imperial synods of the Carlovingian
period which were sometimes combined with diets of
the secular rulers, though not merged in them, as for
instance the *Concilium Germanicum* held under the
influence of St. Boniface in 743. Its decisions were
promulgated as a "sovereign's ordinance" (Capitu-
laries).

Similar developments took place in the Kingdom
of the Visigoths. After the conversion of its kings
from Arianism to Catholicism (third Council of Toledo, 589), the synods of Toledo, eighteen in number
up to 702, were also national synods. In Spain, as
in the Frankish Kingdom, the ecclesiastical and the
civil orders were actually interlocked, though not in
the same way as in the Byzantine Empire. The Visigothic and Frankish territorial or national councils present a faithful picture of this state of things.
They enable us to understand why at this time it
would not have been possible to convoke an ecumenical council in the West. Rome alone was entitled to
do so, but Rome was within the boundaries of the
Roman Empire of the East and did not as yet command adequate influence in the Germanic territorial

churches—apart from the Anglo-Saxon ones, of which it was itself the creator.

Iconoclasm and the Veneration of Images

The onslaught of the Arabs not only tore vast provinces from the Empire of Byzantium, but by the end of the seventh century it reached the very gates of the capital. The military prowess of Leo III, the Isaurian, alone saved Constantinople from capture by the Arabs in 717 and 718. But in 730 the same Emperor, yielding to the persuasion of ecclesiastical circles which were opposed to the veneration of images, and perhaps also moved by Jewish and Islamic precedents, published an edict forbidding the veneration of images (icons). The prohibition was justified on the one hand by an appeal to the Old Testament: "Thou shalt not make to thyself a graven thing," and on the other hand, in so far as the person of Christ was concerned, by the impossibility of expressing his divine nature by means of a picture, while a representation of his human nature alone would be a profession of Nestorianism. This decree led to the senseless destruction of many splendid works of art, while the defenders of the images, as for instance Germanus, Patriarch of Constantinople, were deposed and subjected to a cruel persecution. In vain Pope Gregory III protested against iconoclasm in a Roman synod (731). A synod held at Hieria, on the Bosphorus, sought to bolster up the heresy with theological arguments and finally gave it its approval (754). The Byzantine chronicler Theophanes thus characterizes the decision of its members: "They invested their personal opinions with the dignity of dogmas, on their sole authority, while none of the Catholic episcopal sees were represented, that is, Rome, Alexandria, Antioch and Jerusalem." Constantine V (741-75) raged even more fiercely than his predecessors against

those who upheld the veneration of images. In the
month of August, 766, alone, sixteen higher officials
and army officers were executed on this ground.

The fury of iconoclasm was inspired by political
as well as by religious motives. Resistance to it among
the faithful, and above all in the monastic bodies,
had never died down, but it only gathered momentum
when the energetic Empress Irene took up the regency
during the minority of her son Constantine (780).
Her first attempt to put an end to iconoclasm by
means of a synod proved a failure. On July 31, 786,
iconoclastic soldiers of the imperial bodyguard forced
their way into the church of the Apostles with drawn
swords and scattered the assembly. However, Irene
did not abandon her resolve. With the cooperation of
Tarasius, whom she had promoted to the patriarchal
see of Constantinople and who favored the veneration
of images, she caused an ecumenical council, the
seventh, to meet at Nicaea in the autumn of 787. In
eight sessions, between September 24 and October 23,
the council quashed the iconoclastic decisions of the
synod of 754, refuted the arguments against the veneration of images by other arguments from Scripture
and the Church's own tradition, and drew up the
following doctrinal definition: "Pictorial representations of Christ, of the Mother of God, the Angels and
the Saints, are lawful, for by this means the beholder
is put in mind of their prototypes and encouraged to
imitate them. The cult paid to images (proskynesis)
is related to the prototype and is distinct from the
adoration (*Latreia*) which is due to God alone."
Mild treatment was meted out to bishops who had
held iconoclastic opinions, if they gave proof of a
change of heart. The eighth session, which was also
the last, was held in the Magnaura palace, in the
presence of Irene and her son. More than three hundred bishops, headed by the two papal legates, signed

the acts of the council. "Nothing new was proclaimed," the chronicler Theophanes writes briefly, "only that which had been taught by the holy and blessed fathers was firmly preserved and the new heresy rejected. . . . Peace was restored to the Church of God, even though the enemy never ceases from scattering the seeds of weeds through his satellites. However, the Church is ever victorious, even when she is attacked." As a matter of fact in the ninth century the heresy flared up once more, but only to be defeated finally.

Epilogue in the West

The West had always rejected iconoclasm. Veneration of images was by no means excluded, but they were chiefly esteemed for their didactic value. "Pictures," St. Gregory the Great wrote, "are the books of lay people," by which he meant people who could not read. Whole cycles of Biblical scenes were painted on the walls of churches, as for instance the miracles of our Lord on the walls of the church of Oberzell, on the island of Reichenau. Moreover, the West only knew the Greek text of the acts of Nicaea through a faulty Latin translation in which the distinction made in the Greek text between veneration and adoration was obscured. Charlemagne, who, no less than the Byzantine ruler, saw himself in the role of a guardian of orthodoxy, had the alleged error refuted in a treatise of eighty-five chapters, the so-called *Libri Carolini* —which denied the ecumenical character of the second Council of Nicaea. In 794 Charlemagne countered the heresy with another general council of the West at Frankfort, which was attended not only by bishops of all the ecclesiastical provinces of the Frankish realm and by two legates of the Pope, but even by bishops from England. Charles presided in person, taking, from beginning to end, an active part in the theological discussions. The decrees of the Council of Nicaea of the year 787 were rejected on the ground that they were not ecumenical, but the condemnation did not fully achieve its purpose. Pope Hadrian I (772-95) refused to withdraw his recognition of the Nicene assembly, above all he refused to listen to Charlemagne's demand that he should excommunicate the Byzantine Emperor.

These events, and Charlemagne's coronation as Emperor by Leo III on Christmas Day, 800, show how far apart East and West had drifted by this time. The Rome of the East, within whose jurisdiction the papacy still found itself, had done nothing to relieve the pressure to which it was subjected by the Lombards. Stephen II had accordingly entered into an alliance with Pepin, the founder of the Carlovingian Kingdom, and put himself under his protection. From Pepin he received in return the famous territorial donation which was to develop into the Papal States. Hadrian I was the first Pope who no longer dated his official acts by the years of the reign of the emperors of eastern Rome, the first also to coin his own money. In Constantinople this orientation of the papacy toward the Franks was regarded as a desertion and a treason. It was less than that, and it was also much more. Byzantium, conscious of being the depositary of Graeco-Roman civilization no less than of orthodoxy, and the nascent Christian West, which saw in the Roman papacy and in the Carlovingian imperial authority the two powers on which its ordered life rested, had come apart through something akin to a biological process. The schism between the Latin and the Greek Church, which preceded the eighth ecumenical council, was not caused by the collision between a Pope strongly conscious of his primatial prerogatives and a learned but ambitious patriarch—its causes lay much deeper.

The Photian Schism and Its Settlement By the Eighth Ecumenical Council (869-70)

Pope Nicholas I (858-67) had refused to recognize the Patriarch Photius who had obtained that position after his predecessor had been forced to resign his see. When Photius refused to withdraw and to renounce his claim to jurisdiction over Southern Italy and Dalmatia, the Pope excommunicated him in a Roman synod, in the year 863. The arrival of papal legates in Bulgaria made Photius anxious for his patriarchal prerogatives. He defended himself in a circular letter to the other eastern patriarchs in which he brought grave charges against the Pope and the Western Church. He accused them of tampering with the orthodox faith by the insertion of the *filioque* clause in the Creed, by the doctrine of Purgatory, and so forth. In a synod held at Constantinople in 867 he excommunicated Nicholas I. The schism was a fact.

A few weeks later, in consequence of dynastic changes, when Michael III was murdered and was succeeded by Basil II, the Macedonian, Photius fell from his position and Ignatius was reinstated in the patriarchal see. Not long after these events, on November 13, 867, Nicholas also died. Of him the chronicler Regino of Prüm says that he was "another Elias, by reason of his spirit and strength." The change of persons also brought about a change in the political scene.

Basil II sought the cooperation of the new Pope, Hadrian II (867-72) in the removal of the schism and the reorganization of ecclesiastical conditions by means of an ecumenical council. Hadrian's first step was to confirm the decisions of his predecessor in a synod held at St. Peter's in June, 869. He also appointed three legates to preside at the council convoked by the Emperor and assembled at Constantinople. The legates also insisted on every member of the assembly signing a document which contained a clause expressing submission to the Pope's primacy.

The eighth ecumenical council, the fourth of Constantinople, lasted from October 5, 869, to February 28, 870, during which time ten sessions were held in the church of Sancta Sophia. Attendance was feeble at first but eventually 102 bishops put in an appearance. The Patriarchs of Antioch and Jerusalem sent representatives and from the ninth session onwards a representative of the Patriarch of Alexandria was likewise present. The chief subject of the discussions was the question of Photius and his adherents. In the fifth and seventh sessions, on October 20 and 29, Photius was ordered to appear before the council, but he obstinately refused to plead guilty and contested the juridical competence of the papal legates. The council's sentence was a harsh one: "To the courtier and intruder, anathema." The majority of his adherents shared a similar fate.

The aim of the twenty-seven canons promulgated in the final session was to prevent a repetition of similar occurrences. Canon 3 reaffirmed the lawfulness of the veneration of images. Canon 21 established the order of precedence of the five Patriarchs as follows. First the Pope of Old Rome and after him the Patriarchs of Constantinople, Alexandria, Antioch, Jerusalem. Constantinople's priority over Alexandria, which had been hitherto refused, was a concession on the part of Hadrian II.

The Catholic Church recognizes the assembly of 869-70 as an ecumenical council. Not so the Greek Church. Photius was rehabilitated and at the death of Ignatius he was once more raised to the patriarchal see. A synod assembled by him in 879-80 rejected the decisions of the previous council. The Greeks count this synod as the eighth ecumenical council, but a second schism was apparently avoided. The Papacy, hard pressed by the irruptions of the Saracens into Italy, unprotected by the disintegrating Carlovingian Empire, more and more a plaything of rival factions among the Roman nobility, was about to enter into its darkest period from which it only emerged as a result of the movement for reform which originated at Cluny.

The Greek Church drew new strength from the political and cultural restoration of the Byzantine Empire under the Macedonian Emperors. It consolidated its influence in the Balkans and in Southern Italy, but its greatest success was the adhesion of Russia. A relatively minor dispute over the question of jurisdiction in Southern Italy under Patriarch Michael Caerularius, started a fresh schism which was to prove final. On July 16, 1054, the papal legates Humbert, Frederick of Lorraine and Peter of Amalfi laid on the altar of the church of Sancta Sophia a Bull of excommunication beginning: "Let God witness and judge."

II
THE PAPAL COUNCILS
OF THE CENTRAL MIDDLE AGES

Apart from the council convened by Charlemagne with the object of countering the council of Nicaea of 787, and which he intended to be a national synod of the West, no attempt was made in the early Middle Ages to organize a general council. No claim to ecumenicity was made even by the synod of Sutri in 1046, in which King Henry III put an end to the Papacy's entanglement in the affairs of the city of Rome by removing three rival Popes, thereby forcing open the door for the entrance of the reform movement. Yet this assembly was of momentous import. The general councils of the Middle Ages, to call them by the name by which they described themselves— grew out of the synods which the reform Popes were wont to summon. At first, these synods were attended only by a restricted number of bishops, of whom some came from beyond the frontiers of Italy. They were held either in Rome or in some other locality, and dealt with ecclesiastical affairs of a general nature, but the extent of the area within which their authority could make itself felt was completely dependent on the rise of the reform Papacy and the general recognition of its universal authority. This it only secured after a severe struggle. These assemblies were papal synods in the strict sense of the word.

Papal Reform-Synods and Peace-Council in the Era of the Conflict Over Investitures

After the appearance of the Pseudo-Isidoran decretals, a ninth-century compilation of papal letters, most

of them forgeries, and of conciliar canons, for the
most part genuine, which Pope Nicholas had been too
ready to treat as authentic, it had become a recognized legal axiom in Rome that major synods, that is
such as embraced more than one ecclesiastical province (general synods, though not as yet in the modern
sense of the word), could only be held by papal consent. This is the meaning of the sixteenth proposition
of the celebrated *Dictatus Papae* (the Pope's Dictate)
of Gregory VII, which is as follows: "No synod may
be described as a general synod without his (the
Pope's) decision." As often as synods embracing a
wider circle of participants from different ecclesiastical provinces, or even from different countries, were
convoked, not by legates but by the Pope himself, and
when topics that concerned the welfare of the Church
and Christendom were discussed—such as questions
about the faith, the truce of God, plans for crusades,
or the great problem of the period, the freedom of
the Church—such assemblies gradually acquired an
authority far beyond that of the provincial and national councils of former times. The reform synods
of Pavia and Rheims (1049) convened by Leo IX
(1049-54), the "German" Pope of Lotharingian origin, broke through the limitations of provincial councils. English bishops, among others, were invited by
Leo IX to the Roman council of 1050. At this time,
too, Deoduin, Bishop of Liége, opposed the intention
of the King of France to summon a French national
council for the purpose of condemning Berengarius
of Tours. In the Roman synod of 1059, which was
attended by 113 bishops, Pope Nicholas II (1059-61),
promulgated the famous decree on papal elections,
which reserved the election of a Pope to the cardinals.
The synods of Gregory VII (1073-85) were instru-
mental in the great reforms brought about by this
Pope; namely, the fight against simony, lay investi-

ture and clerical celibacy. These reforms, which gained validity not merely in a limited area, but throughout Christendom, Gregory sought to enforce more stringently than any of his predecessors.[1] To the Lenten synod of 1075 he invited bishops from Northern Italy and France. Those German bishops who were suspected of simony were called to account. Evidence that abbots were invited to such assemblies is found for the first time in the acts of this Pope. He sought to persuade the princes to have themselves represented by envoys so that the secular authorities might take part in the discussion of border questions that concerned them. Both estates of the medieval world, the spiritual and the secular, were to be represented at the synods, under the supreme guidance of the Pope.

In the literature of the conflict over the investitures the role of the councils in the framework of the Church is fully discussed. In the opinion of Bernold of Constance the sentence against Henry IV was "the universal sentence of the Church," because it was not pronounced by the Pope singly (*privatim*), but as president of a general council (*generali concilio praesidens*); a Roman council such as this, though not an ecumenical one, nevertheless has all the appearance of a "truly general synod" (*generalissima synodus*). On the other hand Petrus Crassus, an adherent of Henry IV, insists that the convocation of general councils is a prerogative of the Emperor. The author of the book *On the Unity of the Church,* maintains that this unity is not based on the authority of the Pope over the whole Church, but rather on the unity of the episcopate, as, so he claims, may be read in the writings of St. Cyprian.

These contradictory conceptions explain why the

[1] G. Tangl, *Die Teilnehmer an den Allgemeinen Konzilien des Mittelalters* (1922).

oft mooted plans for a peace council that would end both the conflict over investitures and the schism to which it had given birth, never became a reality. For one thing the Pope would have been made to submit to its judgment, and this Gregory VII would never consent to. He died, to all outward appearances, a defeated man, and in exile, but under his second successor, the French Pope Urban II (1088-99), the papal councils became a triumph for the papacy. In 1095, at Piacenza, before an assembly, it is said, of 200 bishops from Italy, France and Germany, and of thousands of ecclesiastics and lay people, Urban called upon the West to free the Christians of the East from the bondage of the infidels. Later on, but still in the same year, at Clermont, the Pope's inspiring discourse before ninety-two bishops and more than ninety abbots, sounded the signal for the first crusade. Borne by a wave of religious enthusiasm, the Papacy consolidated its ecclesiastical and political position in the as yet undecided fight for the freedom of the Church against the hegemony of the secular powers.

On the other hand we must not lose sight of the fact that the increasing realization of the value of the councils in the course of the conflict over investitures was not exclusively to the advantage of papal authority, on the contrary, it also heightened the bishops' sense of their own importance since the most weighty ecclesiastical decisions in these assemblies were made dependent on their concurrence. According to the teaching of St. Ivo of Chartres (d. *c.* 1116), Pope and council are the joint guarantees of the faithful preservation of ecclesiastical tradition. The bishops' right of playing an active part in these assemblies became apparent at the time when Paschal II (1109-18), in 1111, allowed King Henry V to extort from him the agreement of Monte Mammolo, which conceded to the King the right of investiture with ring and crozier, previous to episcopal consecration, up till now the very thing which Gregory VII had so firmly refused to concede. So decisive was the opposition of the bishops, especially that of the French bishops, that at the Lateran Council of 1112 the Pope found it necessary to withdraw the privilege, *pravilegium*—an evil privilege, as his opponents called it—which he had granted to the King, and to give an assurance that he would abide by the principles of his predecessors Gregory VII and Urban II. The Lateran synod of 1116, which was attended by bishops and abbots, but likewise by dukes and counts from the most diverse countries, among others from Spain, excommunicated the King, although the Pope, by reason of a promise previously made, refused to pronounce the sentence in person. When sentence was pronounced one of those present at the ceremony counted 427 candles in the hands of as many bishops and abbots.

What is evident is that from the time the papacy fell in with the reform movement, both the circle of those who attended the papal councils and the tasks of these assemblies increased steadily. Bishops, abbots, proxies of cathedral clergy of Italy, Germany, France, Spain and England, were invited to attend these synods—even representatives of the laity were there; and the matters discussed and decided upon were the weighty problems of Church reform, papal elections, the investiture of bishops, plans for a crusade, the truce of God.

The First Two General Councils of the Lateran (1123, 1139)

It was, therefore, neither matter for surprise, nor a mere formality, when after the termination of the conflict over investitures by the concordat of Worms concluded with the German King in 1122 (the King renouncing investiture with ring and crozier while safeguarding the interests of the empire) Pope Callistus II (1119-24) was anxious to have this treaty ratified by a council held at the Lateran in the following year. The first Lateran Council, which ranks as an ecumenical one—the ninth in the series—was probably held from March 15 to April 6, at the Lateran, the Pope's cathedral church. The palace adjoining the church, which had been the Popes' residence for a thousand years, contained a conciliar hall, built by Pope Leo III. The hall was directly accessible from the basilica and was adorned with mosaics about which our information is very slender, though we do know that they served a predominantly didactic purpose. The mosaics of the central apse represented Christ, Christ's blessed Mother, and the Apostles Sts. Peter and Paul. The other Apostles were represented in the mosaics of the lateral apses. It may be taken for granted that the discussions of the medieval Lateran Councils were held in this hall while for more solemn events the adjoining basilica would be used. No acts, that is, authentic minutes of the discussions of this first Council of the Lateran, are extant. The same is true of the councils that followed. What we know of these assemblies is gathered from isolated letters of invitation that have been preserved, from references in chronicles, and from their result, that is their decrees and canons. Lists of participants, such as those we possess for most of the early councils, no longer exist. The most credible estimate of the number of the bishops present is three hundred. The number of 997 bishops and abbots given in Pandulph's biography of Callistus II, is undoubtedly an exaggeration.

The twenty-five canons of the first Council of the Lateran are, in part, a reaffirmation of earlier ordinances, such as the prohibition of simony and the maintenance of the truce of God that had been proclaimed at Clermont. Crusaders were granted the remission (indulgence) of the temporal punishment of their sins. Protection was guaranteed to the families they left behind and to their possessions. The robbing of pilgrims to Rome was to be punished with excommunication. The remaining canons dealt with ordinations, the administration of the other sacraments and the appointment to ecclesiastical offices. On March 28, the council witnessed the canonization of Bishop Konrad of Constance (d. 976). Adalbero, Archbishop of Hamburg and Bremen, received the pallium and the Archbishops of Canterbury and York requested the council to settle their dispute over precedence.

The list of agenda shows that this first Lateran Council was already to a high degree the rendezvous and the forum of Christendom. The motive for calling the second Council of the Lateran was a domestic dispute—the schism of Anacletus II.

After the death of Honorius II (1124-30), sixteen cardinals, most of them Frenchmen, elected as Pope the candidate of the powerful Frangipani family, Gregory Papareschi, who took the name of Innocent II. Soon afterwards twenty cardinals elected Peter Pierleoni, "the Pope of the Ghetto," as he was called on account of his Jewish extraction, who took the name of Anacletus II. Anacletus had a powerful supporter in the person of Robert II, King of Sicily. However, St. Bernard of Clairvaux' support of his rival enabled Innocent II to get the upper hand, and this all the more easily as on his two journeys to Rome the Emperor Lothair III took his part and had himself crowned as Emperor by him. Anacletus II nevertheless maintained himself, up to the day of his death, January 25, 1138, in the Vatican and in the Leonine city, that is, the district around St. Peter's situated on the right bank of the Tiber, which Leo IV had surrounded by walls, as a protection against the Saracens.

In the following year (1139) Innocent II, now universally acknowledged, called the bishops and abbots of the West to what he called "a plenary synod" instead of the usual designation—"general synod." The text of the invitation to the distant ecclesiastical province of Compostela has alone been preserved. Once again statements about the number of the participants fluctuate greatly. The annals of Melk on the Danube, refer to 500, while the chronicle of Otto of Freising estimates it at about one thousand. However, even if we accept the lower number as the more likely one, the fact remains that when Otto of Freising described this synod as "a very great one" (*maxima*) he was recording the impression of his contemporaries. Numerous papal documents that were drawn up during this second council show, as in the first Lateran Council, that those who took part in it came from almost every Christian country of the period— from Lincoln in England, Huesca in Spain, and from Jerusalem. However, it was to be expected that as regards numbers, the numerous churches and monasteries of France, Switzerland, Germany and Austria would be the most strongly represented.

The council lasted from April 4, 1139, until the end of the month. In his inaugural address the Pope lamented the confusion caused in the Church by the schism of Anacletus. The latter's adherents were deposed and ordered to give up their palliums, croziers, and rings. To St. Bernard's great chagrin, his protégé, Cardinal Peter of Pisa, also came under this sentence. Most of the thirty canons of the council carry the principles of the reform movement initiated by Gregory VII a stage further, but there are also prohibitions of usury, tournaments and the study of law and medicine by monks. Canon 7 was of particular significance by reason of its bearing on the execution of the law of celibacy, for it did not merely forbid the marriage of clerics, from the subdiaconate onwards, and that of monks, but it also declared them to be null and void. Canon 28 confirms the right of cathedral chapters to elect their bishop, though the authorities that had hitherto been entitled to intervene in these elections were not excluded. This canon became the starting point of the very influential position of cathedral chapters during the Middle Ages.

By this time the range of the council's tasks was even more extensive than in 1123. Canon 23 excommunicated certain sectaries who rejected the Eucharist, infant Baptism, the priesthood and marriage. These men were the heralds of the great heretical movements which before long were to cause so much trouble in the Church. Otto of Freising records that Canon Arnold of Brescia was accused by his own bishop of asserting that an ecclesiastic or a monk who owned any kind of property, could not be saved. On this occasion the Canon escaped lightly—he was only ordered to keep silence.

The second Lateran Council was also the scene of a canonization—that of Sturmius, the first abbot of Fulda, on April 18. But the most influential man of the period, who in fact gave it his name, St. Bernard of Clairvaux, did not assist at the council. The second crusade, which had so unhappy an issue, was the result of his burning eloquence alone. He did not require the assistance of a council.

Conflict and Peace with Barbarossa. Third Lateran Council (1179)

A conflict of a political and ecclesiastical nature, the conflict over investitures, had been the external occasion of the first Lateran Council, and a schism that of the second; both these motives formed the preliminaries of the third.

At the time of the election to the papacy of the Sienese Roland Bandinelli (Alexander III, 1159-81), the Emperor Frederick I, surnamed Barbarossa, mindful of the cardinal's firm attitude at the Diet of Besançon in 1157, had put forward an opposition candidate in the person of Cardinal Octavian of Montecelio (Victor IV). Barbarossa's attempt to restore the imperial authority in Italy caused the cities of Northern Italy to rally to Alexander III's side. The latter refused to appear before the council assembled at Pavia in 1160. It took a bitter struggle of fifteen years' duration before Barbarossa, by the Peace of Venice in 1177, abandoned his antipope, Callistus III, Victor's successor, and undertook to restore all the property of the Church which he had seized. The third Lateran Council, which was foreseen in the peace treaty, set the Church's seal to this act of pacification by which the ascendency of the Papacy was further consolidated. "The council," the Pope said in his invitation to the bishops of Tuscany, "acting in conformity with the custom of the Fathers," would confirm the peace and impart to it an authority which it would not otherwise possess. Alexander obviously links up with the councils of the early Church. What he wanted was to gather round him "the whole world, or at the very least, the whole of the Catholic ecclesiastical world." [2]

The third Lateran Council, the eleventh ecumenical council, is the first for which we have lists of the participating bishops. They furnish 291 names, but the number of those who were actually present probably exceeded 300. The greater part (124), as was natural, was made up of bishops from central and southern Italy, but all the ecclesiastical provinces of

[2] G. Tangl, *op. cit.*

England, Scotland, Ireland, France and Germany were represented either by metropolitans or suffragan bishops. Nineteen bishops came from Spain, five from Dalmatia and eight from the States founded by the crusaders. The number of abbots present is not known, but to judge by the large number of privileges granted to monasteries, it must have been considerable. From an English source we learn that "envoys of nearly every emperor, king or prince in Christendom" were there.

The council held three sessions, on March 5, 7 (or 14) and 19 (or 22), 1179. The chronicler William of Tyre wrote in his *History of the Crusades*: "Those who want to know the decisions of this council, the names, the numbers and titles of the bishops, should read the book which we have written at the request of the members of the synod and have deposited in the archives of our church." But that book has not been preserved. Once again we know next to nothing of the course of the conciliar discussions; all we know is their result, namely, the twenty-seven *Capitula*, of which the first two sum up the dispute that had preceded the council. In order to forestall future schisms, it was stipulated that from this time forward a two-thirds majority would be required for a papal election. The dignities as well as the ordinations conferred by the schismatics were annulled. From the remaining decisions we quote a few typical examples showing the wide range of the authority of the council not only in the ecclesiastical sphere but likewise in the civil one. A candidate for the episcopate must be at least thirty years of age and of legitimate birth— these prescriptions obtain to this day. No one may hold more than one ecclesiastical office or parish, in other words, the cumulation of benefices is forbidden. In every cathedral a schoolmaster must be appointed whose duty it will be to instruct poor students and clerics. Deliveries of weapons and war material, such as iron or wood for ship-building, to the Saracens, was to be punished with excommunication; Jews and Saracens were forbidden to keep Christian slaves. The Cathari, who were numerous in Southern France, were excommunicated. The sentence included those who entertained them, or traded with them. Their property must be confiscated. Men who on the advice of the bishops, take up arms against them, were to enjoy the protection which the Church extended to the crusaders. According to credible information an embassy from the "Poor men of Lyons" presented itself before the council. These people were adherents of Peter Waldes, a former merchant. They had come to submit their translation of the Bible and to seek approval for their lay preaching. They were sent away without being condemned. Only at a latter date did this profession of poverty, inspired though it was by excellent motives, grow into a dangerous sect, scarcely less dangerous in fact than the Cathari who were condemned by the council. Both sects developed into an underground movement. We now realize why the procedure of the medieval councils against heretics differs from that of the early Church. The former regarded heresy not merely as an error in matters of faith, they also regarded it as an attempt to subvert Church and society, hence they were not content with condemning the error but sought to destroy those who taught it.

The chronicler of Stade in Saxony has left us a picture of a homely scene at the council: "At this council," he writes, "the Pope conferred episcopal consecration on two Englishmen and two Scotsmen. One of the latter had come with only one horse, the other on foot with one companion. Among the bishops there was also one from Ireland who told the 'scholasticus' of Bremen that he had no other means

of livelihood than the milk of three cows: when these
went dry the faithful of his diocese replaced them by
others."

The first three Councils of the Lateran obtained
ecumenical recognition owing to the fact that each
of them resolved a burning issue of the time, such as
the conflict over investitures, and the schisms caused
by Anacletus II and Barbarossa. The growing attendance, as well as the intention of those who convoked these assemblies, raises them above the earlier
papal councils. They were, nevertheless, no more than
preparatory steps for the fourth Lateran Council
which was deliberately planned from the beginning
as an ecumenical council. Twelfth in the series of
ecumenical councils, it was held in 1215.

Innocent III at the Fourth Council of the Lateran (1215)

"With desire I have desired to eat this pasch with
you before I suffer" (Luke 22:15). With these words
of our Lord, as if by a presentiment of the nearness
of His death, Pope Innocent III opened the great
Council of the Lateran on November 11, 1215. On
April 19, 1213, "in accordance with the practice of
the ancient fathers," he had invited to this assembly
the eastern and western bishops, the superiors of the
great monastic Orders, the representatives of cathedral
chapters, and the Christian kings. Among the names
of the 404 bishops whom we know to have obeyed
the invitation, we miss those of the Greek bishops of
the Patriarchate of Constantinople, whose presence
had also been requested. Their absence was made
up for by bishops from countries of eastern Europe
which had not been previously represented, from
Bohemia, Hungary, Poland, Lithuania and Esthonia.
Their presence at the council proclaimed the fact that
these countries were part of the Christian West. The

number of abbots is given as eight hundred. The Emperor Frederick II, the Kings of France, England, Aragon, Hungary, the States founded by the crusaders and a few cities, as for instance Genoa, sent their representatives. Thus the whole of Christendom, ecclesiastical and lay, was represented.

Only three sessions were held, on November 11, 20 and 30, 1215. They resulted in seventy "Chapters," as they are called, most of which have become part of Canon Law, but about the manner of their formulation and in general, about the course of the discussions, we are without information. The "Chapters" are headed by a profession of faith aimed at the Cathari, though they are not named. It contains the term "transubstantiation" (change of substance) in the Eucharist, a term elaborated in the course of the discussion of the heretical teaching of Berengarius of Tours, and a condemnation of the teaching on the Trinity of Joachim de Fiore, a Calabrian abbot. The defensive war which the Church had to wage against the heresies of the Cathari, the Waldenses and similar sectaries, is reflected in its prescriptions for the Inquisition. The famous chapter 21, which obliges every Christian who has attained the age of reason to receive the sacraments of Penance and the Eucharist at least once a year retains its binding force to this day. It was a minimum demand but one wholly in keeping with the Pope's determination not to decree anything that was incapable of execution and would, on that account, remain a dead letter.

This sense of reality runs through all the reform legislation of the council. It follows a well-considered plan and includes every degree of the hierarchy and every state and condition of society, and is likewise intended to promote the pastoral ministry. Episcopal sees must not remain vacant beyond a period of three months (can. 23). Owing to the extent of their dio-

ceses, many bishops were not always able to fulfill
their duty of teaching the faith in person. They must
appoint preachers and confessors at their cathedrals
(can. 10). In particular they are urged to see to it
that instructions to the faithful are given in their
mother tongue (can. 9). Annual provincial synods
(can. 6) and general chapters of the religious Orders
(can. 12) must watch over the execution of the reform decrees. In order to raise the standard of clerical education a teacher of grammar must be appointed at the cathedral, and trained theologians at
the metropolitan churches (can. 11). Important
points for the laity were the restriction of marriage
impediments, the prohibition of clandestine marriages
and certain measures to prevent pious frauds in connection with relics and pilgrimages (can. 62). The
legislation for the Jews, such as the prohibition of
their appearing in public during Holy Week, or the
obligation of wearing a distinctive dress, was not
inspired by racial prejudice, nor was it meant to be a
humiliating vexation, for Mohammedans living in
Christian communities were subject to the same regulations. For all that it was so much toll paid to contemporary sentiment.

With Honorius III, the medieval Papacy reached
the climax of its spiritual and secular authority.
Nevertheless, the fourth Lateran Council was not by
any means a mere "display of absolute papal mastery
over the universal Church," nor were the bishops "de-
graded to the role of mere tools of an almighty
Pope," as Heiler would have it. Even Innocent III
did not have his way all the time. A scheme for the
financial security of the papal authorities (Chancery
and Camera), and that of the court, by means of
regular contributions by the whole Church, failed to
obtain the approval of the majority of the council.
It is conceivable that if the measure had been adopted,

the development of the Curia's system of taxation and imposts, which was evolved in the course of the fourteenth century, and which caused so much strife among various nations, would never have come into force. More than one of the council's decrees bears the stamp of the Pope's own forcible personality, but it is, nevertheless, a fact that the reform legislation of the fourth Lateran Council was the result of a genuine cooperation between the Pope and the members of the council. For that very reason it was productive of much good, especially in England, even though the thorough renewal of the Church, which the Pope expected from it, did not materialize. The last hour of the Pope, to whom strangely enough history has denied the title of "the Great," struck on July 16 of the following year; he died at Perugia at the early age of fifty-five.

In virtue of the authority which the papacy claimed and exercised, even in the secular sphere, the council took a certain number of decisions of a secular and political nature, though all of them in some way connected with ecclesiastical interests, as for instance, the conveyance of the county of Toulouse, which was the focus of the Catharist heresy, to Simon de Montfort; the rejection of Magna Charta, which had been extorted from King John; the confirmation of Frederick II as Emperor. The council fixed June 1, 1217, as the date for the start of a great crusade, the rendezvous being the island of Sicily. To meet expenses the clergy were ordered to surrender the twentieth part of their income for a period of three years. In order to keep the available shipping space free for the crusaders, every form of maritime trade with the Mohammedans was forbidden for a period of four years, together with any kind of trade in weapons and warlike material, or personal service in the capacity of pilot on Saracen ships. Large-scale recruiting for the crusade proved a complete success, but the crusade itself, the objective of which was Egypt, the powerful base of every threat to the Holy Places, turned out a complete failure.

The next general council, which Pope Innocent IV assembled at Lyons, carried its intervention in political affairs even further than the fourth Lateran Council.

Deposition of the Emperor Frederick II at the First Council of Lyons (1245)

On the night of June 28 to 29, in 1244, a small group of mounted men made its way, with the utmost haste and in the greatest secrecy, through the wooded territory between Sutri and the harbor of Città Vecchia. Pope Innocent IV, formerly Sinibaldo Fieschi, and a native of Genoa, accompanied only by his nephew, two chamberlains, a chaplain and his confessor, was hastening toward the harbor where a Genoese fleet was waiting for him. He was fleeing from the Emperor Frederick II with whom he had been negotiating for months for a settlement of the conflict which had broken out under his predecessor, Gregory IX, over the respective rights of the Empire and the Church in Italy. The Pope had come to the conclusion that the conflict could not be settled because there was no wish to arrive at an understanding. A ring of imperial troops encircled the Pope and cut him off from all communication with the outer world. When, after his successful escape, the Pope arrived in his home town, Genoa, the people greeted him with enthusiasm, and he quoted the words of the psalmist: "Our soul hath been delivered as a sparrow out of the snare of the fowlers" (Ps. 123:7).

Innocent IV considered that Lyons would be the most favorable ground for the fight against the Emperor on which he was resolved. The city still lay within the boundaries of the Empire, but belonged to its Archbishop and possessed excellent means of communication in the direction both of Germany and France. From Lyons invitations went out on January 3, 1245, to the thirteenth general council. The bishops of France and Spain obeyed the summons in great numbers; a smaller number came from England and Italy and fewer still from the German Empire. Attendance at the council had been very strictly forbidden by the Emperor who also blocked every means of access to it by sea. With an estimated attendance of between 140 and 150 bishops the council of Lyons lagged far behind the most recent council, that of the Lateran.

However, the assembly presents a more colorful picture for us because we have a brief account of its acts, as well as a description in the chronicle of Matthew Paris. In the opening session, on June 28, 1245, in the cathedral of Lyons, the Pope enumerated five wounds under which he suffered. They were—the sins of the clergy, the loss of the Holy City of Jerusalem (it had finally fallen into the hands of the Mohammedans in 1244), the pressure on the Latin Empire of Constantinople (founded during the fourth crusade), the irruption of the Mongols into Europe, and lastly, the greatest concern of all, the persecution of the Church by the Emperor Frederick II. Against him the Pope made the gravest accusations, such as heresy, an alliance with the infidels, breach of contract and perjury. The president of the supreme court of justice, the Sicilian Thaddeus of Suessa, defended his master shrewdly and objectively, but Innocent refuted his arguments one by one. One of the accusations was connected with the council which Innocent had intended to convene in the Lateran, at Easter 1241. Frederick prevented the assembly by intercepting the Genoese fleet which was carrying a hundred prelates, who were all made prisoners.

A week later, in the session of July 5, the proceedings against the Emperor were resumed. Thaddeus of Suessa was unable to refute the accusation that Frederick had used violence against bishops, but a postponement of the sentence for a period of twelve days was granted by the Pope, to enable Thaddeus to obtain fresh instructions from his master.

During that interval the council disposed of divers problems of the Church. Of its twenty-two "Chapters" (not seventeen or eighteen as was thought at one time) eight were in reality decisions of an earlier date, which the council merely confirmed. Previous to his elevation to the papal chair Innocent IV had held the chair of Canon Law at Bologna, a circumstance that accounts for his interest in the reorganization of the Church's legislation with regard to judicial procedure. Some of the "Chapters" are concerned with this subject. But the great problems of Christendom, of which the Pope had spoken in his inaugural discourse, were not forgotten.

The Pope himself undertook to defray the cost of the fortifications with which it was hoped to ward off future irruptions of the Mongols. Non-resident holders of benefices were ordered to contribute one third of their annual income for the support of the Latin Emperor of Constantinople, and as at the fourth Lateran Council, all ecclesiastics were commanded to surrender a twentieth of their income for the reconquest of the Holy Places in Palestine.

These decisions were approved in the third session of the council, held on July 17, in which a deputation of English peers lodged a protest against the bestowal of English benefices on Italians. The protest was unsuccessful. However, the most important subject of the discussions was the sentence against the Emperor. As a perjurer, a disturber of the peace and suspect of heresy, a sentence of deposition from his dignity of German King and Roman Emperor was pronounced against him. This was the first deposition of an emperor by a Pope since the days of Gregory VII. "O day of wrath, distress and lamentation," Thaddeus of Suessa exclaimed. In point of fact the day marked the beginning of the downfall of the Hohenstaufen and the decline of imperial power. It was also undoubtedly a trial of strength on the part of papal fulness of power in the secular sphere to which, in the long run, the Papacy proved unequal.

A little over a month after the final session of the council, August 25, 1245, Innocent IV forwarded the twenty-two "Chapters" of the council to the universities "for use in the administration of justice and for instruction," thereby giving them force of law. Together with eleven other decrees they were embodied in the definitive collection of papal laws published in 1253. The procedure throws light on the relation between Pope and council; we shall have to return to it when we come to the next council.

The Crusade, Reunion with the Greeks, Organization of the Conclave at the Second Council of Lyons (1274)

The second Council of Lyons, the fourteenth ecumenical one, had been preceded by a prolonged vacancy of the Holy See. For nearly three years after the death of Clement IV, on November 29, 1268, the cardinals, split up as they were into parties, had failed to agree upon a single candidate. In order to force a decision the citizens of Viterbo removed the roof of the episcopal palace where the electors resided. On September 1, 1271, their choice fell on Tedaldo Visconti of Piacenza, who was at that moment at Acre, the Christians' last bulwark in the East. It was to be expected that the cause of the crusade—in reality a lost cause by this time—would be very near his heart. "Jerusalem, Jerusalem, should I ever be unmindful of

thee," are said to have been his last words on his
departure from the Holy Land. But he was no less
keen on reunion with the Greeks, who had recon-
quered Constantinople and overthrown the Latin Empire, but who feared a counter-attack by King Charles
of Naples.

The papal election, the crusade and reunion with
the Greeks were to be the main themes of the council which Gregory X convoked in the month of April
1273. It was to meet once again at Lyons. Invitations
were sent not only to archbishops, bishops, cathedral
chapters and abbots—only one of the latter from each
diocese—but the kings and princes of the West were
likewise invited, as well as the Greek Emperor Michael
of Constantinople, the King and the Katholikos (the
ecclesiastical head) of Armenia, and even the Great
Khan of the Mongols, reports of whose leanings toward Christianity, exaggerated though they surely
were, had reached the West. Though attendance at
the council did not equal that of the fourth Lateran
Council, it, nevertheless, bore a real resemblance to
it on account of the international character of its
membership. Next to Italy, Germany was most
strongly represented, for all its six archbishops and
twenty-eight bishops were there. France was represented by thirty-one bishops; the Spanish peninsula
and England sent twenty-five prelates each—a grand
total of over two hundred prelates whose presence can
be established with complete certainty. The estimates
of the chroniclers, which include abbots and other
dignitaries, as well as the proxies, rise to a thousand
and even beyond. One of the invited, the greatest of
them all, was missing: Thomas Aquinas had died
while on the way from Naples to Lyons, on March 7,
1274, in the convent of Fossanuova, near Rome. His
was the same fate as St. Augustine's who died before
the Council of Ephesus.

The second Council of Lyons was opened on the Monday of Rogation week, May 7, 1274, with a sermon by Gregory X, based on the same Scripture text as that quoted by his predecessor, Innocent III, at the opening of the fourth Council of the Lateran: "With desire I have desired to eat this pasch with you . . ." (Luke 22:15). He then spoke of the three-fold object of the Council, namely, the relief of Jerusalem, union with the Greeks, the reform of the Church. The cardinal-bishops sat on the right of the Pope, among them St. Bonaventure, the cardinal-priests on his left, with the archbishops, bishops and abbots on either side of them. The Latin Patriarchs of Constantinople and Antioch occupied special places in the nave of the church, a sign that there was no intention as yet to subordinate the patriarchial dignity to the cardinalate. Special places were likewise assigned to King James of Aragon and to the envoys of the Kings of France, Germany, England and Sicily, and to the representatives of the religious Orders of knighthood.

In order to raise the money for a large-scale crusade the Pope judged it necessary to ask for a contribution four times higher than that which Innocent III had asked for, nemely a tenth for six years. Thanks to his shrewd tactics in the course of the discussion, he succeeded in wresting from the prelates a reluctant assent. He did not treat with them in a plenary assembly, but negotiated separately with the representatives of each ecclesiastical province. By the time the second session was held, on May 18, the expressions of assent had all come to hand. In the interest of the crusade the Pope prescribed the preservation of peace for a period of six years: however, even before the crusade could be organized Acre had fallen, May 8, 1291.

June 24, witnessed the arrival of the Greek envoys.

They were the former Patriarch of Constantinople, Germanus, the Archbishop of Nicaea and the logothete (chancellor) of the Emperor. In the fourth session, July 6, they accepted the prescribed profession of faith which contained the recognition of papal primacy, the doctrine of Purgatory and the septenary number of the sacraments. On behalf of their Emperor, the deputies sealed the union of the Greek Church with the Church of Rome with an oath. During the Mass which followed the Creed was sung in Latin and in Greek, with the *filioque* clause. After the Greeks had confessed their faith in the *filioque* in this way, they were given permission to retain the traditional text of their Creed. The union did not last, because the Emperor had only supported it from political motives and the Greek hierarchy would not hear of it. But there was yet another reason, none other than the fact that Pope Martin IV (1281-85) supported the King of Naples' plans of conquest in the East.

The famous decree on papal elections *Ubi periculum*, which was accepted in the fifth session, held on July 16, and which, with only slight alterations and enlargements, remains in force to this day, was based on the model of the election of magistrates in a number of Italian cities. It ordains that ten days after the Pope's death the cardinals must assemble for the election of a successor, in complete seclusion from the outer world (conclave). Should the election not be completed after three days, they are to have only one dish both for their midday and their evening meal; should five more days go by they are to have nothing but bread and water. During the whole duration of the conclave they are to lose the revenues contributed by the Church. The Council accepted this law for papal elections in spite of the cardinals' not unnatural resistance.

Even before the Council the Pope had asked that memoranda should be submitted on the reform of the Church which he planned. At least three of these documents have been preserved, among them that of the general of the Dominicans, Humbert of Romans. To what extent they led to a definite course of action we can only conclude once more from the final result of the discussions. Some of the thirty-one "Chapters," the majority of which were accepted in the third session, June 7, and in the fifth and sixth, held on July 16 and 17, are concerned with episcopal and other ecclesiastical elections. The extensive pastoral activity of the four mendicant Orders founded in the course of the thirteenth century—the Dominicans, Franciscans, Hermits of St. Augustine and Carmelites, met with all manner of opposition from the secular clergy. Canon 23 confirmed their privileges but failed to put an end to the tension. Every successive council, up to that of Trent, had to deal with the problem.

On November 1, 1274 the conciliar decisions were given force of law by Gregory X, though after a few minor alterations. This is a striking proof of the fact that the Pope claimed and exercised supreme authority over the council.

Both by reason of its personnel and the whole character of the assembly, the second Council of Lyons resembled the fourth Lateran Council. The resemblance was also due to the fact that both assemblies took measures of a political nature. The dispute for the German crown between King Alfonso of Castile and Rudolf of Habsburg was decided, in principle, when the Pope accepted the promises by which Rudolf bound himself, and summoned his rival to renounce his claim. The formal recognition of Rudolf took place after the termination of the council, on September 26, 1274. Thus ended an unhappy interregnum. King James I of Aragon, who had come to the council for the purpose of having himself crowned by the Pope, departed in high dudgeon because Gregory insisted on his doing homage to him and paying him a vassal's fees. The King of France surrendered the county of Venaissin which had long been the Pope's property, but had been administered up to this time by a vassal. A deputation from the Great Khan of the Mongols vainly endeavored to bring about an alliance against Egypt. However, one of its members asked for Baptism. Repeated attempts to carry Christianity to the Far-East by taking advantage of the toleration which the Mongol Khans extended to it, proved a failure, in spite of some astonishing achievements, as for instance those of the Franciscan Giovanni de Montecorvino. The cause of the failure was, in the end, the fact of distance. The breadth of planning and the determination that radiated from the person of Gregory X upon the council remains a permanent object of wonder and astonishment. The Church venerates him as one of her *Beati*.

The Shadow of Boniface VIII

Two decades later, in the masterful personality of Boniface VIII, the Papacy attained to the apex of its power. In the Bull *Unam Sanctam,* this Pope formulated a theory which, though not really new, was nevertheless characteristic of that particular period. This was the doctrine of the two swords in the hands of the Pope, one spiritual, the other temporal, one wielded *by* the Church, the other *for* the Church. Boniface's conflict with the King of France, Philip the Fair, and his kidnaping by the king's emissaries at Anagni, on September 7, 1303, constituted the first move in a new epoch of the Papacy, the "exile" of Avignon. The personality of Boniface VIII cast its shadow even over the council which his second successor, Clement V, convoked on August 12, 1308. The

locality of the assembly was to be Vienne, on the
Rhone. The invitations were sent out from Poitiers
where the Pope had had a meeting with Philip the
Fair. The subjects of discussion enumerated in the
Bull of convocation were the affair of the Order of
the Templars, questions connected with the faith, the
reform of the Church, and the recovery of the Holy
Land. Contrary to custom, not all bishops were
called to the council; a selection was made—one previously discussed with the King of France. This
revealing circumstance shows to what a condition the
Papacy had been reduced by this time. One of the
two lists of bishops who were selected, known as the
Paris list after the place where it was found, contains
165 names; the other, the definitive one, contains 231
names. Twenty cardinals, four patriarchs, twenty-nine
archbishops, seventy-nine bishops and thirty-eight abbots complied with the invitation. The French and
the Italians constituted the largest party, but the presence of the Archbishops of Taragona, Braga and Compostela, York, Armagh, Dublin, Cologne, Magdeburg
and Bremen shows that "the whole of the episcopate
was undoubtedly represented at the council." [3] A
number of absentees had themselves represented by
proxies. The Council of Vienne was still a bishops'
council, but to some extent it was also a proxies'
council.

"Many things here vex me. The place is uncom-
monly cold and in view of my advanced years this
circumstance causes me much inconvenience. A crowd
of people is pressed together in this small town. This
too creates a vast amount of inconvenience. However,
we must have patience." These expressions of resignation are found in a letter of Bishop Raymund of
Valencia who represented James II of Aragon, and
were written in the city of the council on November

[3] E. Müller, *Das Konzil von Vienne* (1934).

9, 1311, to the bishop's sovereign. Three weeks earlier, October 16, Clement V had inaugurated the fifteenth ecumenical council at Vienne.

The Liturgical Ceremonial of the Opening Session at Vienne (1311)

The sessions of the general councils are not merely juridical acts of the Church, they are also liturgical functions, like a canonization or the coronation of a Pope. Their liturgical form is more than a decking out of these assemblies as with a garment, it is, on the contrary, of their very essence, as the promulgation by them of binding decisions on questions of faith and discipline is an act of religion and therefore directly concerned with the service of God.

The opening session of the Council of Vienne on October 16, 1311, shows already the identical liturgical structure with which we shall meet again at the Councils of Constance, Basle and Trent. Certain divergences at Vienne were solely due to the circumstance that the Pope was present in person.

Clement V, wearing pontifical vestments, made his entry into the cathedral with only a small following and took his seat on the throne prepared for him in the sanctuary. The Latin Patriarchs of Alexandria and Antioch had places by themselves in the center of the church. The rest of the prelates, wearing copes and linen mitres, sat in three rows, one above the other, in the main nave, one hundred and fourteen mitred dignitaries in all. After the Pope had given his blessing the cantors intoned an antiphon. At the deacon's bidding (*Flectamus genua*) all fell on their knees. When he rose again, the Pope, turning toward the assembly, recited the prayer to the Holy Ghost prescribed by the Ordinarium: *Adsumus Domine.* "We are gathered here O Lord, in thy name. Come to our aid, be with us. . . ." After this prayer all knelt down once more and the Litany of the Saints was sung. This was followed by a second collect, also said by the Pope. The Cardinal-deacon, Napoleon Orsini, sang the gospel which recounts the mission of the seventy disciples (Luke 10:1-16), which had been sung at the second Council of Lyons and which was to be sung two hundred years later at Trent. The Pope then intoned the hymn *Veni Creator Spiritus,* which was taken up by the whole assembly and sung right through.

These ceremonies were no more than preliminaries, for it was only at this stage that the Pope delivered his opening discourse in which he unfolded the program of the council. It comprised three points. The question of the Order of the Templars, the reconquest of the Holy Land, the reform of morals and the freedom of the Church. In his conclusion he announced the formation of a conciliar commission whose task it would be to examine the affairs of the Templars but, contrary to custom, he mentioned no date for the next session. The whole ceremony ended with the papal blessing.

Such was the opening of the Council of Vienne. At later councils, at which the Pope did not preside in person, the opening ceremony described above was usually preceded by the Mass of the Holy Ghost and a sermon by a member of the assembly. Instead of the Pope's opening discourse there was an address by the president. This was followed by the decision to open the council, expressed by the *Placet* of the members entitled to a vote, and in subsequent sessions, by the reading and approval of the decrees. The votes (*vota*) were registered by collectors who went from one member to another and, on occasion, also received explanations or qualifications of the votes written in the voter's own hand (*schedae*). The session regularly ended with the *Te Deum.*

The Trial of the Templars
and Church Reform

The opening of the Council had been delayed for a whole year owing to the trial of the Templars, an Order of Knighthood, which was to be brought to a conclusion in this assembly. The Order of the Templars had been originally founded for the defense of pilgrims to the Holy Places, but after the loss of the Holy Land their proper task had come to an end. Their great wealth was the motive, and the moral disorders which undoubtedly existed among them, provided a pretext for the decree of the King of France, Philip the Fair, on October 13, 1307, for the arrest of all the members of the Order in his kingdom, and for the confiscation of their property. To describe the manner in which the order was executed one is tempted to say that it was done by means of a *Blitzkrieg*, but for the fact that the expression has acquired a more sinister meaning in the last war.

The act was a flagrant breach of Canon Law, to which the Order was subject. Even after Clement V had taken charge of the trial and appointed a papal commission of enquiry, he was unable to shake off pressure by the king, a pressure rendered yet more crushing by the latter's demand for the posthumous trial of his mortal enemy, Boniface VIII. Throughout the trial Philip used this demand as a means of bringing political pressure to bear on the Pope. The judges appointed by the Pope insisted that judgment in the trial of the Templars could not be pronounced on the basis of the data of the Inquisition, some of which had been extorted by the rack, but that the Order must be given an opportunity to defend itself. The prolonged discussions which went on throughout the winter of 1311-12, did not end in a judicial sentence by the council, but in the suppression of the Order by an administrative act of the Pope, on March

22, 1312, two days after Philip's arrival at Vienne. But the property of the Order was not assigned to a new Order of Knighthood, yet to be founded, as Philip had demanded, and through it to himself; on the contrary, it was granted to the Knights of St. John. The suppression of the Order was made public in the second session, April 3, 1312. The trial of Boniface never took place.

The two constitutions on the observance of poverty in the Order of St. Francis and on the teaching of the Franciscan, John Peter Olivi, which were promulgated in the third, and last session, May 6, 1312, had a long history behind them. The school of the so-called "Spirituals," who appealed to the spirit of the founder, St. Francis, reproached the majority of the Order with the abandonment, on the strength of papal privileges, of the primitive ideal of poverty. On the other hand, the majority attacked the orthodoxy of one of the leaders of the "Spirituals," Olivi. An investigation by a commission of cardinals and bishops of the council, resulted in the exoneration of the majority, but directives were given for a practical realization of the ideal of poverty (*usus pauper*). Three doctrines ascribed to Olivi were condemned, but without his name being mentioned; one of them was the opinion that the human soul was not the "form" of the body.

In order to obtain data for the discussion on reform, Clement V had urged the bishops to draw up memoranda on the abuses that might exist in their dioceses. Two sets of problems emerged from the copious material obtained by this means—first the complaints (*gravamina*) of the interference and the encroachments in the ecclesiastical sphere by the secular power, for instance with regard to the special juridical position of the clergy, its immunity from taxation, the administration of Church property and hospitals; and secondly, the obstruction of the bishops' authority by exemptions, that is, the freedom from episcopal jurisdiction granted by the Popes to cathedral and collegiate chapters, individual monasteries and entire religious Orders. The first set of grievances was a consequence of the growing power of the State, while the second arose out of the centralization of authority developed by the Roman Curia. "Out of a total of thirty-five benefices attached to my cathedral, which became vacant during the twenty years of my work as bishop, I have been able to dispose of only two," was the lament of Bishop Lemaire of Angers. When we go through the lists of episcopal grievances, we find an enumeration of almost all the abuses which came up for discussion at the councils of the fifteenth and sixteenth centuries. This is the same as saying that the reform decrees which were accepted in the final session did not produce a lasting effect. On October 25, 1317, John XXII, Clement V's successor, after yet another revision, forwarded them to the universities and gave them force of law. They constitute a substantial part of the so-called *Clementinae,* or *Liber Clementinarum*, and form an addition to the *Corpus Iuris Canonici*. Our conclusion is that the Pope felt justified in editing the decisions taken at the council, in revising them where necessary, and finally enforcing them.

The crusade also was discussed once more. But it soon became apparent that the idea of a crusade, that is, of a fight against the infidels, was on the decline whereas the missionary idea was in the ascendant. On the initiative of the philosopher Raymond Lully (Ramon Lull) the Council of Vienne, by the so-called "canon of languages," prescribed the setting-up at the universities of chairs of Greek, Hebrew, and Arabic, on the ground that acquaintance with these languages was a prerequisite for missionary work among Jews and Mohammedans. The canon was put into practice in only a few universities owing to lack of teachers.

The far-reaching suggestions for a reform which Durandus, Bishop of Mende, expounded in his voluminous *Tractatus de modo concilii generalis celebrandi,* namely a systematic strengthening of episcopal authority and a simultaneous curtailment of papal administrative methods, the organization of synods on the model of those of the early Church, the raising of the level of clerical training, made no headway at Vienne but they portended the advent of a new epoch.

"The council stood at the crossroads of two worlds." [4] The papal general councils of the second half of the Middle Ages had been the work of the reform Papacy. All of them had been convoked, and presided over by the Popes. Like the early councils they were bishops' councils but enlarged by the participation of abbots, representatives of cathedral chapters and even of the secular power. Though the latter were not entitled to a vote (strictly speaking) they had the right of making themselves heard in matters that concerned them. The Pope gave their final form to the conciliar decrees and embodied a large number of them in the papal code of laws. At the councils he appears as the head of the Church and of all Christendom, as the apex of the pyramid which included both the Church and the community of all Christian peoples. All this was changed when the councils came to be regarded as the "representation" of Christendom and of all the members of the Church, for whom constitutional rights were claimed. At a time when the Papacy went through a period of weakness the attempt to enforce these claims was actually made.

---

[4] E. Müller, *op. cit.*

III
THE COUNCIL
ABOVE THE POPE?

THE Council of Vienne was the last papal council of the central period of the Middle Ages. At that time ideas were already being aired which ascribed to the general councils a far more extensive role than any they had hitherto fulfilled. There was question of nothing less than that the council, as the final and supreme authority, should restore the unity of the Church in spite of a Papacy split into two, and carry out an urgently needed reform of the Church both in her head and in her members (*reformatio in capite et membris*).

Origin of Conciliar Theory

The doctrine that the council was superior to the Pope, commonly described by the expression "conciliar theory," was at one time traced back to Marsilius of Padua (d. 1342), the exponent of revolutionary theories of the sovereignty of the people, and to his follower William of Ockham (d. 1349). The reasoning seemed simple enough. Just as the State is created by the will of the people, and is built up from below, so is the Church. Her hierarchy, the Pope and the bishops, was not founded by Christ, it is only the result of an historical process. Ecclesiastical authority, restricted to the preaching of the word of God and the administration of the sacraments, is vested in "the body of the faithful." The general council "represents" (renders present) the Church and is superior to every grade of the hierarchy, including the Pope.

We know now that this derivation of conciliar theory from Marsilius and Ockham, which we have deliberately simplified in order to make it perfectly clear, does not correspond to historical reality. Above all the notion of "representation" is older than Marsilius and owed nothing to him for its development. It had its roots in the notion of the Church as a corporation, made up of head and members, which perform joint functions but each of which has its individual rights and duties. Contrary to the claims of the strict curialists, the Pope is not the sole depositary of all power in the Church, on the contrary, according to the Dominican John of Paris (d. 1306), who is the chief exponent of this theory of the Church, authority rests not with the head alone but extends also to the members. The latter, through the election of the Pope by the cardinals, transfer their rights to these dignitaries; however, it is open to them to rescind this transfer should the Pope err in a matter of faith or abuse his power to the detriment of the Church.

Beneath this theory of the Church there lies a yet earlier one, that goes back to the canonists of the twelfth century. Huguccio (d. 1210), a canonist of Bologna and Innocent III's teacher, maintained that the Pope might err personally, the Church never. By the term Church must be understood, in the first instance, the Roman Church, and after that the universal Church as the totality of all the faithful. But who is to prove that the Pope is in error in a matter of faith? The obvious answer would be: the council as the representation of the whole Church. However, thus far the canonists were not prepared to go, because they shrunk from ascribing to the council judicial power over the Pope, which would be in direct opposition to the legal axiom: "the Pope cannot be judged by anyone." The most the council could do was to establish the fact that the Pope had erred, but in that case, they maintained, the erring Pope would *ipso facto* cease to be Pope. To get out of the dilemma they argued in this way: When the Pope makes a decision in a matter concerning the faith, he is bound by the advice of the bishops; if he seeks this advice in a council, which represents the Church, he cannot err. This co-operation of council and Pope is expressed by the axiom: the council (with the Pope) is greater than the Pope (by himself alone).

These trends, which originated in the central period of the Middle Ages and led to conciliar theory, were reinforced by historical facts in which opposition to the doctrine of the Pope's fullness of power becomes apparent. When Boniface VIII took action against the refractory cardinals of the house of the Colonna, the latter appealed to a general council. The aim of Philip the Fair's coup at Anagni was to force the Pope to submit to the anti-papal council he was contemplating. The appeal of the Emperor Louis the Bavarian, at Sachsenhausen, against the sentence pronounced by John XXII, was based on the legal opinion that it was lawful to appeal to the general council from a sentence pronounced by a Pope who exceeded his prerogatives.

The Great Schism of the West

What these conceptions of the council as the "representation" of the Church meant in practice only appeared when on September 20, 1378, a group of

cardinals, dissatisfied with Gregory XI's return to
Rome from Avignon, as well as with the autocratic
character of his successor Urban VI, elected Cardinal
Robert of Geneva as antipope and returned with him
to Avignon, thus placing themselves under the protection of the King of France. Thereafter two Popes
faced each other, together with their adherents—
their "obediences."

The Great Schism of the West differed from most
previous schisms in that no secular power had anything to do with it, at least not directly, as had been
the case in the schism of Barbarossa. In the present
instance it was the majority of the legitimate electors
of the Pope who declared the election of Urban VI
invalid, on the ground that it was a forced one, on
account of the violence of the Roman populace, hence
the new election was alone valid. Who, then, was the
rightful Pope? Urban VI or Clement VII? and who
was to decide the question of legitimacy?

"The General Council," was the answer of two
German theologians who taught at the University of
Paris. As early as 1379, Henry of Langenstein and
Konrad of Gelnhausen maintained that in the existing emergency a General Council representing the
whole Church was the judge both of the cardinals
and of the two Popes elected by them. In 1393, in a
memorandum drawn up in its name by Nicholas of
Clémanges for Charles V, King of France, the University of Paris advocated a solution by means of a
council, should it prove impossible to obtain the spon-
taneous resignation of both Popes, or to persuade
them to submit to arbitration. Two decades were to
elapse before recourse was had to a council. This
goes to show that the basic principle of conciliar
theory was still very far from having attained the
strength and the general recognition with which its
antecedents might lead one to credit it. It was only

after attempts made by the Neapolitan Boniface IX in Rome after 1389, and by the Spaniard Benedict XIII at Avignon after 1394, had failed to bring about an understanding between the rival Popes, and when his repudiation by France had also failed to shake Benedict XIII's conviction that he was in the right, that thirteen cardinals who had broken both with him and with the Roman Pontiff, Gregory XII (1406-15) convoked, from Leghorn, a general council for the purpose of putting an end to the disastrous schism. The council was to assemble at Pisa on March 25, 1409.

The Council of Pisa: Three Popes Instead of Two

The legal basis of the Council of Pisa was extremely insecure because, at the very least, the cardinals of one of the two obediences who issued the convocation could not be legitimate. Two days before the opening, on March 23, 1409, at Heidelberg, the German King, Rupprecht the Palatine, lodged a protest against the Council of Pisa. However, he could not prevent the convocation from proving, at least initially, a complete success. Close on a hundred archbishops and bishops and as many abbots accepted the invitation. To them came to be added the proxies of over one hundred bishops, two hundred abbots, one hundred cathedral chapters and thirteen universities. One third of the members of the council were Frenchmen. Gregory XII and Benedict XIII were summoned to appear before the council as obstinate heretics. When they failed to do so they were declared obstinate and were deposed on June 5, 1409. Previous to this step the assembly, in the eighth and ninth sessions, had constituted itself an "ecumenical council." On June 26, with the authorization of the council, the cardinals present elected as Pope the

learned Franciscan Peter Filarghi, a native of the Isle
of Crete, who took the name of Alexander V. However, behind him there already loomed another figure,
that of Baltassar Cossa, the energetic and unscrupulous
legate of Bologna, who succeeded the Greek in the following year under the name of John XXIII. "The
odious dualism has been replaced by an accursed
trinity," we read in a contemporary tractate, for even
after the election of Pisa both Gregory XII and Benedict XIII continued to claim that they were the legitimate holders of the papal dignity, although their
"obediences" had shrunk considerably. Both of them
had countered the council of Pisa with poorly attended
opposition synods at Cividale (Friuli) and Perpignan respectively. Gregory counted among his adherents, besides King Rupprecht, only Naples, Venice and
Malatesta, Duke of Rimini; Spain and Scotland sided
with Benedict. The Pope elected by the council had
the largest following, but his legitimacy was doubtful
and remained uncertain. Thus the first attempt to
restore the unity of the Church ended in failure.

Convocation of the Council of Constance
By King Sigismund and
Pope John XXIII (1414-18)

If success was eventually achieved by means of a
council, credit is due, in the first place, to the German
King Sigismund (1410-37), a prince possessed of a
nimble but erratic mind, who, nevertheless, gave proof
of astonishing skill and great perseverance in connection with the council. He broke with the policy of his
predecessor, embraced the part of John and wrested
from him a reluctant assent to a great council of reunion in the imperial city of Constance, on the Lake
of the same name, which he announced on October
30, 1413, in a proclamation addressed to the whole
Christian world. On his part, too, John XXIII subse-

quently issued an invitation on December 9, 1413. By means of negotiations with the two other Popes and with nearly every European State, Sigismund made certain in advance that the attendance would be truly ecumenical. The Emperor of Constantinople, Manuel, also received an invitation.

John XXIII regarded the Council of Constance as a continuation of the Council of Pisa. He cherished the hope that it would confirm him in office. Gregory XII had been abandoned by almost the whole of Italy, and the Italians constituted the majority at Constance, so John's prospects were not unfavorable. However, within a few months after the opening, on November 5, 1414, a change came over the assembly. In order to prevent their being outvoted by the Italians, the English, the Germans and the French demanded that the voting should not be individual but by nation. The demand was agreed to with the result that each of the four "conciliar nations" had one vote, irrespective of the number of its members. The College of Cardinals had the fifth vote.

Voting by nations was an exclusive peculiarity of the Council of Constance. It was not, as might be suspected, a break with the national principle. The conciliar nations were combinations inspired by political considerations, bodies debating and voting jointly and which admitted various nationalities. In this they resembled the "nations" of the medieval universities. The German conciliar nation, besides the Germans, also included the Scandinavians, the Poles, the Czechs, the Hungarians, the Croatians and the Dalmatians. The English nation included the Scots and the Irish. As at Pisa, the bishops and abbots personally present formed a minority against the proxies of the absentees and of the ecclesiastical corporations (monasteries, chapters, universities), as well as the doctors of theology and Canon Law.

Flight and Deposition of John XXIII

Soon after Christmas sundry complaints of the
Pisan Pope's conduct were heard in the council. In
point of fact, John XXIII's mode of life was not altogether blameless. He realized that his hope of confirmation by the council was not likely to be fulfilled.
He accordingly declared himself ready to resign,
though under certain conditions. At the same time
he was making secret plans of escape by which he
hoped to wreck the council. Even before the opening
of the assembly he had come to an understanding
with Frederick, Duke of the Tyrol, with a view to
his personal safety. Trusting to this arrangement he
made his escape in disguise, mounted on a small horse
"uff einem kleinen rösly," as the chronicler put it, to
Schaffhausen, on March 20, 1415. The council had
been formally convoked by him; was it going to col-
lapse? It almost looked as if it would. John had
many adherents, among them eight cardinals. Many
tradesmen, both natives and strangers, packed up their
goods for fear of their shops being plundered, while
the burgomaster called the burghers to arms. Sigismund alone saved the situation. Accompanied by the
Count Palatine, Louis, he rode through the town,
"calling at the houses of the money-changers, whether
Italians or of any other nation, the shopkeepers and
tradesmen, the cardinals and other lords, ordering a
proclamation to be made, and calling out with his own
mouth that no one was to leave." [1] On March 23, the
chancellor of the University of Paris, Gerson, spoke
at length, on the basis of conciliar theory, of the
consequences of the situation. "Every member of the
Church," he declared, "must obey the general council, even the Pope. The council cannot abrogate papal
supremacy, but it can restrict it if the welfare of the

[1] See Chronicle of Ulrich von Richental (ed. M. R. Buck,
1882).

Church requires it. Christ's union with the Church is indissoluble—not so the Pope's."

These were the basic ideas which the council, on April 6, formulated in the famous decree *Sacrosancta* (from the opening word): "The ecumenical council assembled at Constance represents the whole Church. It derives its authority immediately from Christ. Everyone, even the Pope, owes obedience to it in all that concerns the faith, the unity of the Church and the reform of both head and members."

We must always bear in mind that this decree owes its origin to the situation created by the Pope's flight from Constance. It was regarded as an emergency measure. Its content was in keeping with conciliar theory, but it met even then with opposition from some of the cardinals. Pierre d'Ailly, the most influential of the French cardinals, did not attend the session and his colleague and fellow countryman, Fillastre, refused to read the decree. It was, nevertheless, accepted by the council. The heaviest crisis was thus overcome. On May 17, John XXIII was taken to Radolfzell as a prisoner; on May 29 he was deposed.

Resignation of Gregory XII — Deposition of Benedict XIII

The two other Popes continued to cling to their positions. Gregory XII, whose conduct had been the most correct, was now forsaken by nearly everybody. Dietrich von Niem indulged in a cheap kind of pun at his expense by turning his family name Correr, Correrius in its Latinized form, into *Errorius*—roughly a "blunderer." Gregory stuck to the very end to his claim that he was the legitimate Pope. In the fourteenth session, on July 4, 1415, he submitted, through his protector Malatesta of Rimini, a document by which he offered his resignation, but not before he had legitimized the council by a new Bull of convocation. He took his place once more in the College of Cardinals and died two years later as Cardinal-Bishop of Porto.

The Avignon Pope, Benedict XIII, proved much more intractable. After France had abandoned him, he had migrated into the dominions of the King of Aragon. Accompanied by a deputation of the council, Sigismund had an interview with him at Narbonne in August, 1415. Benedict did not absolutely refuse to resign, but promised to do so on condition that the Council of Pisa was declared null and void and the Council of Constance transferred to another locality, one that would be acceptable to himself. His first demand was accepted, but not the second. When Sigismund urged him to resign he replied, according to the chronicle of his adherent, Martin of Alpartil: "You say that neither I myself nor my opponent (Gregory XII) is Pope. In that case not one cardinal is in existence except myself (he was the only cardinal of the last Pope before the schism), so I alone have a right to elect the Pope. If you wish it, I shall elect him within twenty-four hours, and I also promise you that I shall not elect myself." This demand, so characteristic of a strict but rigid legal mentality, was likewise refused. When he realized that the only thing for him to do was to resign, he fled from Perpignan, accompanied by a handful of adherents and retired to the impregnable mountain-fortress of Peñiscola, where he declared: "This is Noah's ark; here is the true Church." His adherents dissociated themselves from him by the Treaty of Narbonne, December 13, 1415, as did the Kings of Aragon, Castile, Navarre and Portugal, who had supported him until then. Spain had itself represented at Constance, thereby constituting the fifth conciliar nation. Proceedings against Benedict were started, but in view of his blameless

life, his obstinate refusal to resign was the only charge
against him. Sentence of deposition was pronounced
on July 26, 1417.

The Election of Martin V

The way was now clear for the election of a new
Pope. The cardinals at Constance declared their will-
ingness to allow representatives of the conciliar nations to take part in the election. But the council
itself threatened to split up over the one great question: Should the reform of the Church be decreed
before the election and its observance imposed on the
future Pope—as the English and the German nations
demanded and the Emperor Sigismund strongly urged
—or should not the schism be first eliminated, after
which the task of reform could be initiated? So great
was the shock of different opinions that the council
came to the very verge of dissolution. In the end the
defection of the English compelled the Germans to
give way. The Bishop of Winchester, a cousin of
King Henry V of England, obtained approval for a
compromise. It was to the effect that the papal election should take place immediately, but that the reform decrees already drawn up should be first promulgated while a conciliar decree should bind the
future Pope to carry the reform further.

The most important among the five reform decrees
which were accepted in the thirty-ninth session, held
on October 9, 1417, was the decree *Frequens*, so called
from the initial word, by the terms of which general
councils were constituted a permanent institution of
the Church and for that reason were possessed of a
controlling authority over the Papacy. The next two
councils were to be convoked five and seven years
respectively after the conclusion of the present one,
and after that there was to be one every ten years. If
this decree had been carried into effect, the general

councils would have developed into a permanent institution and by this means the revolutionary principle
of the decree *Sacrosancta* would inevitably have become operative.

On November 8, 1417, fifty-three electors entered
the conclave prepared for them in the *Kaufhaus*
(Merchants' Hall) at Constance, the College of Cardinals having been reinforced by six deputies from
each of the conciliar nations. The Frenchmen's hope
of securing the tiara for their countryman d'Ailly
faded away. On November 11, Cardinal Oddo Colonna, a member of the ancient and powerful Roman
family, needed only one vote for a two-third's majority. At that moment a procession of intercession was
passing by in the street and a large body of boys was
singing the *Veni Creator Spiritus*. The chant sounded
like an angelic choir. Thereupon two more cardinals,
with tears in their eyes, gave their votes to Colonna.
"Before the processional cross re-entered the minster,"
Ulrich von Richental records, "people outside the
conclave began to shout: 'We have a Pope—Oddo
Colonna,' and everybody rushed to the Merchants'
Hall, close on eighty thousand persons, both men and
women." Their joy was justified—the Church had
once more an undoubtedly legitimate Pope.

Church Reform and Concordats

The power of the idea of the Papacy made itself
felt immediately after this successful election. Martin
V was from the first the unquestioned head of the
council; but he had the wisdom to follow the advice
of four of the most influential bishops of the council,
namely, the Archbishop of Milan, the Patriarch of
Antioch, the Archbishop of Riga and the Bishop of
Salisbury, the first letter of whose titles produced the
anagram: Mars rules the council.

But the freedom of the council was by no means

in such straits. On the other hand the suspicion of
the English and German nations, that the reform of
the Church would not come about after the election,
proved correct, though the chief blame for this lay not
with the Pope but with the disunity of the would-be
reformers. On one thing they were all agreed, namely,
that the Pope's fulness of power should be curtailed
as much as possible, but they disagreed about the
measures by which this could be effected. The wishes
of the conciliar nations, as stated in their *Avisamenta*,
differed widely and Peter von Pulka, a Viennese professor, accurately judged the situation when he wrote:
"At the moment, I fear, there will be no serious reform." True, in the forty-third session, on March 21,
1418, seven reform decrees were completed and an
attempt was made, for instance, to reduce the number of the cardinals to twenty-four, to reduce papal
interference in the system of offices and benefices (by
means of exemption and incorporations which greatly
hindered the bishops' work), to what it was before
the schism. The most important problems of all were
not settled once for all, and by the authority of the
council, but by means of conventions between the
Pope and the conciliar nations. The concordats of
Constance, unlike the concordats of modern times,
were not conventions between Church and State, but
simple agreements between the Pope and the conciliar nations, for a period of five years (with the
exception of the English one which was to be permanent), and dressed up as papal constitutions. Their
theme was: the approval by the Pope of episcopal and
abbatial elections, the restriction of reservation of
benefices and the concession of indulgences and the
payment of annates (that is, fees payable to the Curia
on preferment to offices). However, no one had any
illusions about the nature of a declaration that accompanied the acceptance of the seven reform decrees and

the concordats. By this acceptance, it said, the reform decided upon previously to the papal election, had been adequately honored. The declaration was a mere formality. Before long it became abundantly clear that the longing for a genuine reform had not been satisfied.

The Trial of John Hus

It was precisely such a renewal of the Church that had preoccupied John Hus, a professor of Prague, whose teaching and person occupied the council during the period of discussions that followed the deposition of John XXIII. Like his prototype, John Wyclif, whose forty-five theses had been condemned on May 4, 1415, Hus sought to escape from the existing Church, so lamentably afflicted with countless ailments, into the spiritual Church of the divinely predestined, in which participation in Christ's redemption is guaranteed, not by an official priesthood and the material administration of the sacraments, but solely by the possession of the Spirit. While his personal life was blameless, Hus had exasperated even his former patron, the Archbishop of Prague, by his unsparing criticism of the clergy, but in return he had gained a large following among the nobility and among the Czech population. The council was to speak the last word on his case.

The Emperor Sigismund had granted Hus a safe-conduct for the journey and the sentence of excommunication had been rescinded, though not that of suspension, that is, the prohibition to say Mass and to preach. When Hus ignored this prohibition while at Constance, he was placed under arrest. When confronted with the judges appointed by the council to investigate his case, he refused to retract his teaching: "I teach no error," he said, "no Czech is a heretic." On July 6, 1415, he was condemned as an obstinate heretic and in accordance with the law then in force, handed over to the secular arm for execution. A year later he was followed to the stake by his friend Jerome of Prague who had at first recanted. The steadfastness with which he met his death drew from the humanist Poggio who witnessed the execution, the remark: *Vir praeter fidem egregius*—Apart from his belief a splendid man.

In the same session which condemned Hus, the council also rejected the opinion of the Franciscan Jean Petit who taught that it was lawful to assassinate a tyrant regardless of any oath of loyalty to him. This condemnation of the murder of a tyrant, though based on quite specific assumptions and conditions of time, has been effective right up to our own time.

"The Council of Constance," Cardinal Fillastre observes at the end of his diary, "was more difficult to convoke than all the previous councils; its course was also more singular and more wonderful, and at the same time more perilous than theirs; finally it surpassed them by its duration." Fillastre was right; the Council of Constance lasted longer than all previous councils, most of which accomplished their task within a few weeks or months. However, this council was faced with a task the gravity of which exceeded any that similar assemblies had ever had to deal with. This fact also accounts for its questionable concessions to conciliar theory. No council had ever brought together so lively and so varied a group of men. The Minnesinger Oswald von Wolkenstein, mindful of the dearth and dearness of provisions at Constance, wrote this verse: *Denk ich an den Bodensee, tut mir gleich der Beutel weh*—"When I think of the Lake of Constance, my purse immediately hurts me." A gathering of over three hundred cardinals, bishops and abbots, the court of Sigismund and that of a number of princes with their suites—approximately 15,000 to 20,000 strangers in a town of less than 10,000 inhabitants, was bound to force up prices. In the streets of Constance every language of the then known world could be heard. The council became a center of exchange for the life of the spirit. Italian humanism entered upon its forward march, to its own benefit, when its exponents explored the libraries of the monastic houses of the district along the shores of the Lake of Constance, in search for the works of classical writers. Thus Poggio found a copy of Plautus in a convent of nuns. However, the council's most important achievement was the restoration of unity to the Church, though that unity was weighted with a heavy load. Conciliar theory, the offspring of a state of emergency in the Church, continued to proliferate, although it could never fit into the hierarchical structure of the Church. The Church is indeed democratic, from the point of view of the equality of all men before God, but she is not a democracy.

Martin V gave no formal approval to the decrees of Constance for the simple reason that the majority of the council, influenced as it was by conciliar theory, would scarcely have accepted such an approval. His statement in the forty-fifth session, that he approved all the decisions passed by the authority of the council, refers only to the affair of the Dominican John Falkenberg. However, the Pope condemned conciliar theory indirectly when he expressly forbade appeal from the Pope to the council. On the other hand he complied with the decree *Frequens*. After the lapse of the five-year period he opened a new council at Pavia, as had been agreed upon at Constance, but transferred it to Siena and finally closed it because it was only feebly attended. Seven years later he convoked another council to Basle. He did so reluctantly and solely under the pressure of veiled menaces.

Eugenius IV and the Council of Basle

A contest between the Pope's primatial authority and conciliar theory was inevitable. On the other hand we may well ask whether it would have taken so dramatic a turn and one so dangerous for the Papacy if, with all his piety and benevolence, Martin V's successor, Eugenius IV (1431-47), a nephew of Gregory XII who had withdrawn from his position, had been less undecided and less dependent on the men around him. The bishops had not recovered from their weariness of councils. The Council of Basle, the seventeenth ecumenical one, was inaugurated on July 23, 1431, by the representatives of the papal legate Cesarini, though not a single bishop was present. Up to the month of October attendance was so feeble that the Pope felt justified in closing the council on December 18. But what had been feared already at Siena, now became a reality—the council refused to obey. When the Bull dissolving the assembly was about to be read, the members left the hall. Cesarini relinquished the office of president. The decree *Sacrosancta* was renewed; the Pope was requested to rescind the order for its dissolution; he was even called to account by the council. This was the time when the profoundest thinker of the period, Nicholas of Cues (Cusanus), on the Moselle, wrote his *Concordantia Catholica* in defense of the council. The council had powerful protectors in the persons of King Sigismund and of Visconti, Duke of Milan. The conflict lasted two years; at the end of that time, Eugenius gave way. Some of the cardinals had disapproved of the overhasty dissolution from the beginning; St. Frances of Rome advised the Pope to withdraw it. The number of the Pope's adherents decreased with every passing month and the *condottiere* Fortebraccio suddenly invaded the Papal States. On the other hand the council was able to register a great success. On

November 30, 1433, the Hussites, who by their predatory invasions had become the scourge of the neighboring countries, and who had defeated several armies of crusaders that had been sent against them, accepted the *Compactata* of Prague which granted to them, on certain conditions, Communion in both kinds, together with some other concessions. Eugenius IV accordingly withdrew the decree of dissolution on December 15, 1433, and declared that the Council of Basle was to be regarded as a legitimate assembly. The victory of the men of Basle seemed complete.

In the meantime the council had started to put conciliar theory into practice and to constitute itself the supreme judicial and administrative authority in the Church. It appointed its own staff of officials, gave judgment in lawsuits, granted benefices and indulgences. To an even greater degree than Constance, the Council of Basle was an assembly of proxies and doctors. In a vote taken on December 5, 1436, three cardinals, nineteen bishops and twenty-nine abbots were faced by three hundred and three other participants at the council; the bishops, therefore, formed much less than a tenth of the participants. Any member of the council had a right to a vote and could be elected to any one of the four committees dealing with general questions, faith, reform and peace. A head-committee issued directions and guided the whole system. By reason of its order of procedure the council was not unlike a modern parliament, in fact it was so even by its tendency to claim for itself ever more business, and by this means the real guidance of the Church.

Prompted by a great number of memoranda about reform, among them a most original one by the Bishop of Lübeck, Johann Schele, the council promulgated between the year 1433 and 1436, some remarkable decrees about Church reform which, if they had been

carried into effect, could have made a valuable contribution to the reform of the Church. They dealt
with such matters as the regular holding of provincial
and diocesan synods, the liturgy of the Church, clerical concubinage and unjustifiable appeals to Rome.
But some of the decrees clearly tended to control
papal authority and to appropriate executive power
to the council, as for instance the complete abolition
of the payment to the Roman Curia of the annates and
all other taxes. This measure would have deprived
the Curia of the greater part of its income without
any compensation. The council directed the papal
collectors to give an account at Basle; new regulations for the election of a Pope were likewise promulgated.

Eugenius IV, who had escaped only with difficulty
from a revolutionary outbreak in Rome, was residing
at Florence. In August, 1435, he protested against
these acts through the General of the Camaldolese,
Traversari, and again in the spring of 1436 through
Cardinals Albergati and Cervantes—but without any
success. A breach between Pope and council finally
came in the summer of 1437, on the question of the
locality of the forthcoming council of union with the
Greeks.

Definitive Rupture Between Pope and Council

The Emperor John VIII Palaeologus, pressed as he
was by the Osmanli from both East and West, sought
an alliance with and help from, the West, a prerequisite of which he rightly judged would be the restoration of ecclesiastical communion with Rome. To this
end he opened negotiations with the Pope and with
the council. For a locality for such a meeting the
council suggested either Basle or Avignon, while Eugenius IV proposed Udine or Florence. It was not an
edifying spectacle when two rival western embassies

set out for Constantinople. When on May 7, 1437, after a long debate this way and that, the conciliar majority decided in favor of Basle or Avignon, while the minority favored the Pope's choice, the latter sided with them. The Greeks accepted the Pope's proposal and agreed with him on Ferrara, which was favorably situated from their point of view. On September 18, 1437, the Pope transferred the Council of Basle to that city. The minority, among them Cardinals Cesarini and Nicholas of Cues, obeyed the decree ordering the translation, the majority remained at Basle.

There the adherents of conciliar theory gained the upper hand and threw off every restraint. They proclaimed the council's superiority over the Pope as an article of faith. Eugenius IV, who could not but reject such a claim, was deposed by them on a charge of heresy, June 25, 1439. On November 5 of the same year they elected in his place Duke Amadeus of Savoy (Felix V), whose personal conduct was irreproachable and whose wealth commended him to the choice of the council which was in financial straits. Conciliar theory, which at Constance had contributed to the elimination of the Great Schism, produced a new schism at Basle, the last in the history of the Papacy. This was its greatest blunder.

Council of Union with the Greeks at Ferrara and Florence

Meanwhile Eugenius IV's position had been strengthened by a great success. The council of union with the Greeks had been inaugurated on April 9, 1438, in the cathedral of Ferrara, in presence of the Pope and of more than seventy bishops of the West, the Byzantine Emperor, Patriarch Joseph of Constantinople, the Archbishops of Ephesus, Nicaea and Kiev, as well as the representatives of the Patriarchs of

Alexandria, Antioch and Jerusalem. The controverted doctrines between Latins and Greeks were discussed by committees in such wise that the Greeks stated their objections to the standpoint of the Latins, to which the latter replied. Even before any result had appeared Eugenius IV found himself obliged, for lack of money—(he had undertaken to provide for the seven hundred Greeks who assisted at the council)— to accept an offer of the city of Florence which would relieve him of his financial burden and to transfer the council to that city, January 16, 1439. There agreement was reached, first on an addition to the Creed which had proved a recurrent cause of contention ever since it was first inserted in the *Credo* in the Carlovingian era, namely, the clause *filioque* by which we confess that the Holy Spirit proceeds from the Father *and the Son.* Then, secondly, there was agreement, though after long and heated disputes, on the most difficult of all the controverted points, the doctrine of papal supremacy, namely, that the Apostolic See and the Pope are invested with supremacy over the whole world. As the successor of St. Peter and Vicar of Christ the Pope is the head of the whole Church, the father and teacher of all Christians and possesses authority to guide the whole Church, in accordance with the acts and canons of the ancient councils. This last clause the Latins understood as merely explanatory while the Greeks interpreted it in a restrictive sense. The Bull of union *Laetentur coeli*, the original of which is still extant, was read in the session of July 6, 1439, by Cardinal Cesarini in Latin, and by Bessarion, Archbishop of Nicaea, in the Greek text. The former bears 115 signatures, the latter 33, headed by that of the Emperor.

A Russian, who had accompanied the Archbishop of Kiev to Florence, explained the Latins' joy over the union after his own fashion: "They rejoiced because they had been pardoned by the Greeks." The union did not last because the Greek clergy's dislike of the Latins was greater than their fear of the Osmanli. When Mehmed the Conqueror attacked Constantinople in 1455 the West did not rouse itself to concerted action.

In the same way the union concluded soon afterwards with the Armenians (November 22, 1439), as well as the later one, in 1442, with the Monophysite Armenians, did not affect these autocephalous Churches in their entirety. On April 25, 1452, the council was transferred to Rome.

Termination of the Schism of Basle

The successful union with the Greeks was a victory for Eugenius IV in his contest with the Council of Basle, but it was, nevertheless, far from being a final victory. True, the following of the anti-pope was very small, consisting as it did of only Switzerland, Austria, a part of Bavaria, the University of Paris and a few other universities. Much more dangerous was the neutrality of France and Germany. As early as May and June, 1438, a national assembly at Bourges had decided to remain neutral in the dispute between Pope and Council. At the same time, on its own authority, it gave force of law to some of the reform decrees of Basle. (Pragmatic sanction of Bourges in which the superiority of the council over the Pope was acknowledged.) Even before this the German Electors had proclaimed their neutrality at Frankfort. A year later the German episcopate followed the example of the French hierarchy and accepted some of the decrees of Basle as obligatory.[2] England, Burgundy and Venice stood by Eugenius IV. The greatest danger, therefore, did not lie in the schism itself, but in this

[2] Instrument of Acceptation of Mainz, 1439.

policy of neutrality based on conciliar theory. However, the rump-council which upheld it, by its own
progressive radicalism, deprived itself of any prestige
it might have enjoyed. Straitened by financial difficulties, it transferred itself in 1443 to Lausanne, the
residence of the anti-pope. One country after another
returned to the obedience of Eugenius IV—Hungary,
Aragon, Castile, Scotland, Poland. Enea Silvio Pic-
colomini, the former secretary to the council, but by
this time in the service of the Emperor Frederick III,
won his new master over to Eugenius. At the Diet of
Frankfort in 1446 the Germans also came round and
concluded the so-called princes' concordats with the
Pope, against an assurance that he would convoke a
new, "third" council to a German city. These concordats were followed on February 17, 1448, as their
final result, by the concordat of Vienna, but by this
time the partner in the transaction was Eugenius IV's
successor, Nicholas V. This concordat resembled the
concordats of Constance, but was to remain in force
for all time. When France also abandoned her neutrality Felix V resigned on April 7, 1449.

Eugenius IV owed his final victory over the Council of Basle as much to its mistakes as to the altered
policy of the secular powers which were disquieted
by the radicalism of the schismatics. He also had at
his side a number of outstanding personalities of the
College of Cardinals—men like Cesarini, at one time
president of the council, Albergati, Capranica and
Nicholas of Cues, while Cardinals Vitelleschi and
Scarampo had strengthened his position in the States
of the Church. In his great *Summa* on the Church,
Cardinal Torquemada gave fresh expression to the
conception of the primacy. However, conciliar theory
was not yet completely eliminated, were it only that
council and reform continued to be closely linked together in the mentality of the period.

Survival of the Idea of the Council

The champions of an idea may be defeated, the idea itself only vanishes from history when it is defeated by another idea. A moderate form of conciliar theory was upheld by the great canonist of the period, Nicholas Tudeschi, Archbishop of Palermo—hence his name *Panormitanus*. It was also taught at many universities, for it was one way of viewing the Church. Those who thought a reform of the Church could not be effected except by a council were both numerous and ranked among the best. The Carthusian, James of Jüterbogk, was of the opinion that the Church would never be reformed by the Pope alone. The attempt of the Dominican Andrew Zamometic, in 1482, to re-open the Council of Basle which had never been formally closed, was the desperate act of an adventurer and proved a failure. But the only road by which conciliar theory would have been made really powerless, namely, a serious start of the long-delayed reform of the Church, the Papacy did not take. For this neglect the admirable achievements of the Papacy of the Renaissance in the sphere of culture were no compensation, all the more so as they were accompanied by a further development of the Curia's fiscal system and by undeniable symptoms of corruption.

On the other hand the Popes' disinclination to organize councils grew all the more as the threat of a council became a current political weapon. King Louis XI of France and Podiebrad of Bohemia made use of it against Paul II and Sixtus IV, Charles VIII of France and Ferdinand of Aragon against Alexander VI. But the threat became a reality only when Louis XII of France, in his war against Julius II, made use of a handful of disgruntled cardinals to convoke an antipapal council at Pisa in 1511, the so-called *conciliabulum* of Pisa. Those who took part in it were almost all of them Frenchmen and the King of France was their only support. They gained little by renewing the well-known decrees of Constance. At the beginning of 1512 they betook themselves to Milan. The *conciliabulum* of Pisa would not be worth mentioning had it not decided Julius II (1503-13) to convoke on his part a general council for April 19, 1512. This was the fifth Lateran Council (1512-17).

The Fifth Council of the Lateran (1512-17)

The last Council of the Lateran, the eighteenth ecumenical Council, consciously conformed to the pattern of the papal councils of the central period of the Middle Ages, and thus differentiated itself from the two councils of the preceding century. Held as it was in Rome, under the eyes and under the presidency of the Pope, it was attended almost exclusively by Italian bishops. At the opening session on May 10, 1512, fifteen cardinals and seventy-nine bishops were present. The Pope himself fixed the order of procedure and he also named all the officials. The decrees took the form of papal Bulls.

The council's immediate task was to invalidate the Pisan opposition council. This proved comparatively easy. Already in the second and third session, May 17, and December 3, 1512, respectively, the Kings of England and Aragon as well as the Emperor Maximilian, declared themselves in favor of the Roman council and against that of Pisa. Louis XII also dropped it after the death of his opponent, Julius II (February 21, 1513), and the rebellious cardinals made their submission to the newly elected Pope, Leo X. The Papacy's relations with France were regulated in 1516 by a fresh concordat which was approved by the council in the eleventh session held on December 19, 1516. The only dogmatic definition of the fifth Lateran Council, in its eighth session on

December 19, 1513, was aimed at the philosopher Peter Pomponazzi (without mention of his name); it defines the immortality of the individual human soul.

The chief question for the council was whether it would command sufficient courage and determination to undertake a serious reform of the Church. "Men must be changed by holiness, holiness must not be altered by men," so spoke the general of the Augustinians, Aegidius of Viterbo, in his sermon at the opening of the council. In 1513, soon after Leo X's election, two Camaldolese, Giustiniani and Quirini, submitted to the Pope a memorandum on Church reform which had not its like as regards the frankness of its criticism of abuses, while it did not exhaust itself in mere criticism; on the contrary it was brimfull of positive proposals. These included a revision of Canon Law, uniformity in the religious Orders and in the liturgy, resumption of the negotiations for union with the eastern Churches and even the missions in the recently discovered New World.

The aims of the fifth Lateran Council did not go thus far, but it promulgated a small number of most useful reform decrees, for instance in the eighth session, on the Curia's system of taxation; in the ninth, which took place on May 5, 1514, on the choice of bishops, religious instruction and the security of Church property; in the tenth, May 4, 1515, on the *montes pietatis,* non-profit pawnshops, for which there was a pressing need in this era of early capitalism, and the censoring of books; in the eleventh session, about preaching. During the discussion of the latter subject the bishops' resentment of the privileges of the mendicant Orders vented itself in vehement complaints and accusations. But on the whole it remains that it was precisely in respect of the worst abuses—the cumulation of benefices, the neglect of the duty of residence, the policy of *laissez-faire* of so many ecclesiastical persons, that the council failed to take strong measures without which no change could be brought about. The inflammable material that had accumulated especially in the North was not rendered harmless. The demand voiced in a Spanish memorandum "Judgment must begin in the house of the Lord" remained unheeded. Not even the modest content of the Lateran decrees was quickened into life and reality, for there was no strong will to carry them through consistently, no firm purpose to prevent their being weakened by readily granted dispensations. Leo X, the son of Lorenzo the Magnificent, was no reform Pope. The Lateran Synods of the Middle Ages could not be revived in an altered world. The fifth Lateran Council was closed in its twelfth session, on March 16, 1517. On October 31 of the same year Martin Luther nailed his ninety-five theses to the door of the court-church of Wittenberg.

IV
THE RELIGIOUS DIVISION
AND THE COUNCIL OF TRENT

"Everybody shouts: A council, a council!" the papal nuncio Aleander wrote from the Diet of Worms (1521) where the affair of Luther was about to be discussed. While his trial was still in progress and subsequent to the fruitless examination by the Cardinal-legate, Thomas de Vio, of Gaeta, at Augsburg (1518), the young Augustinian friar had appealed to a better informed Pope and to a general council, regardless of the fact that the prohibition of such appeals by Martin V had been renewed by Pius II, Sixtus IV and Julius II, and further strengthened by a clause that invalidated them. On the advice of the jurists of Wittenberg Luther had made a second appeal after he had been informed of the Bull *Exsurge Domine* of June 15, 1520, which threatened him with excommunication. At that time the appeal was no more than a legal maneuver for only a year before, in the course of his disputation at Leipzig with Johann Eck, he had described the judgment of Hus by the Council of Constance as unjust and, when driven into a corner, he had declared that even general councils may err. Even then his last and only standard of faith was Holy Scripture (*sola Scriptura*).

For all that he strongly upheld the usefulness of reform councils. In his book published in the same year 1520 "To the Christian nobility of the German Nation," he urged the "nobility," that is the princes and secular Estates, to take the reform of the Church into their own hands, if need be at a council. "Therefore," he wrote, "if need demands it and the Pope gives scandal to Christendom, he who is able to do so, as a true member of the whole body, should see to it that a truly free council is held, which no one is so well able to bring about as the secular sword." Luther drew up a comprehensive program of reform for a future council which agreed largely with the criticism of the Roman Curia and other abuses in the Church that are found in his earlier writings about reform, while it differed from them by the fact that he ascribed responsibility for the injuries of the Church not so much to the moral failure of men, as to the adulteration of the true Gospel, for which, in his opinion, the Papacy and Aristotelian scholasticism were chiefly to blame. What he called "reformation" was something very different from the efforts for reform during the central period of the Middle Ages, including even those of the upholders of conciliar theory. Luther's idea was that as soon as the Gospel, the light of which, he alleged, had become obscured, began to shine once more, and justification by faith alone was proclaimed, the Church would recover its true "form," it would in fact be "reformed."

The condemnation by the Pope of forty-one theses extracted from Luther's writing, was not regarded by many who were still influenced by conciliar theory, as the Church's last word. A general council could alone speak such a word. "Luther was in the Church and remains there; he can only be excluded from it if he is condemned by a judicial sentence pronounced by a general council." This marginal note of the

syndic of Augsburg, Konrad Peutinger, put into words
what was in the mind of wide lay and even ecclesiastical circles. For all that nearly a lifetime went by
before such a council came together. The cause of
this delay was the change which the idea of the council had undergone, and also in the political opposition
between the two great powers—the Habsburgs and
France.

A "General, Free, Christian
Council in German Lands"

At the Diet of Worms a solution by means of a
council did not get under way, not only because Luther was unwilling to submit unconditionally to the
decision of a general council, but equally so because
the Pope's representative, Nuncio Aleander, did not
give it his support, though from very different motives. On the other hand the conviction that a general council alone was qualified to speak the last word
on what was true and what was false in Luther's
teaching, was so widespread, that at the following
Diet, at Nuremberg, all the Estates of the Empire,
both Catholic and adherents of Luther, demanded
a "general, free, Christian council in German lands."

The formula sounded harmless enough; but, at least
as conceived by the Lutherans, it disguised demands
which were bound to encounter strong objections on
the part of Rome. For one thing, the word "free"
meant "independent of the Pope." Since the Pope was
a party to Luther's affair, he could neither convoke
the council nor preside over it—the assembly must be
convoked jointly by the Emperor and the Christian
princes. "Christian" meant that not only bishops and
clerics, but laymen also were to take part in it and to
have a right to vote. The council must be a "Christian" one, that is, its judgments must be exclusively
based on the Scriptures. The demand that the coun-

cil must be held on German soil was based on the fact that the dispute to be settled had broken out in Germany. It was for this reason that the ancient councils of the early centuries were all held in the East.

It is evident that this interpretation of the formula of Nuremberg went far beyond the mutations which the idea of the council had undergone in the course of the middle and later centuries of the Middle Ages. In the light of the history of the councils its revolutionary character is clearly revealed.

This explains why the formula gave rise to strong misgivings in Rome. By this time Clement VII (1523-34), Leo X's cousin, had become Pope. He shared his predecessors' aversion to a council, not only on account of the events of Constance and Basle which cast a dark shadow over all the preliminaries of the Council of Trent, but likewise for personal reasons which were not due to his own ethical conduct but to the circumstance of his illegitimate birth. Throughout his reign, though he never uttered a clear "No," Clement VII sought to ward off and to by-pass the demand for a council. He felt that there were other means to arrest the movement of apostasy; he had faith in the magic of diplomacy.

The task of preventing a German national council was made easy for him. Since Rome was obviously determined to remain passive, the council was to be convened at Speyer, in accordance with a resolution of the second Diet of Nuremberg, in 1524. In the end the Emperor forbade it. Yet the same monarch, at this time still youthful and guided, in the political sphere, by his Grandchancellor Gattinara, was eventually to become one of the most ardent champions of a solution by means of a council. Writing in the third person he says in his Memoirs: "Since the Emperor's first journey to Italy in the year 1529, and his meeting with Pope Clement and Pope Paul, and after that as often as he met Pope Clement and Pope Paul, as well as at every Diet held by him, and at all other times and on every occasion, either personally or through his ministers, he never neglected to urge the convocation of a general council. When he says this, he speaks the truth." In 1530, when on his way from Spain to Germany, Charles had himself crowned as Emperor of Bologna. While there he wrested from the Pope a conditional assent to a council, namely, in the event of the failure of the attempt to bring about an agreement with the Protestants. As a matter of fact the great Diet of Augsburg failed in its efforts for such an agreement. For all that, in Clement VII's mind the objections to a council vastly outweighed its advantages, hence he tied up its convocation with every kind of condition. The preliminary negotiations became bogged. The Pope had the support of the King of France, Francis I, who feared that a council and the removal by its means of the religious dispute in Germany would increase the power of his political opponent, the Emperor Charles.

France maintained her negative attitude, or at least her waiting policy, even after the successor of the second Medici Pope, Paul III (1534-49), a scion of the house of Farnese, had given the Emperor, on the occasion of the latter's visit to Rome in the spring of 1536, a firm assent to the convocation of a council, a promise which he fulfilled on June 2 of the same year. The extraordinarily shrewd Farnese Pope, whose character we are better able to know through Titian's incomparable portraits than by means of any written description, had long ago realized that the pressure of public opinion could not be resisted any longer. The council and the reform of the Church constituted the main points of the program of his pontificate. This position they retained even though in the course of the years, especially the later years, he increasingly felt the risks inherent in a council and the sacrifices which a serious reform would demand of him. The result was that his general attitude became more and more hesitant. Only with reservations may he be described as the first Pope of the Catholic reform.

The Failure of Mantua and Vicenza

The first convocation to a council at Mantua, on May 23, 1537, proved a failure. As a fief of the Empire that city met one of the conditions laid down by the Germans, but the failure was due not only to the outbreak of a fresh war between Charles V and Francis I, which rendered France's assent, already feeble, ineffective, but likewise to the Duke of Mantua's demand that if the council was to be accommodated in his capital city, a guard of between five and six thousand men would have to be raised and its pay guaranteed. With the consent of Venice the Pope accordingly directed that the council should meet at Vicenza. Three papal legates were named, namely, Cardinals Campeggio, Simonetta and Aleander. They set out for Vicenza but attendance, even from Italy, remained exceedingly feeble. A few representatives of some German bishops came and left again, while the German Protestants, who since 1531 had formed a political and military alliance known as the League of Schmalkalden, bluntly declined the invitation to Mantua which had been communicated to them by nuncio Peter van der Vorst. The opening was put off from day to day and on May 21, 1539, it was finally adjourned *sine die*.

This issue of the plan gave great satisfaction to the King of England, Henry VIII, who by the act of supremacy of 1534, had severed his connection with the Roman Church, for he feared that a general council might lead to the formation of a hostile continental league. On the other hand, the Catholics of Germany, whose numbers were steadily declining, felt bitterly disappointed. In Protestant circles it was openly said that the Pope did not really want a council—all he wanted, as the Lutheran Corvinus insinuated, was to "cock a snook at the kings and at all the world."

Such was not his intention; in fact it was precisely with a view to the council to which he had agreed, that Paul III, in the autumn of 1536, invited to Rome a reform commission of nine prelates, among them the newly-created Cardinals Contarini and Carafa. On March 9, 1537, the commission submitted a memorandum "on the cleansing of the Church" which on the score of clarity left nothing to be desired and advocated the application of the most drastic measures to the administrative methods of the officials of the Curia and to the whole life of the Church. Thereupon sub-commissions were formed for the reform of the papal Chancery, the Camera, the Penitenzieria and the Dataria, the most violently criticized department of all. As to the motive, no doubt is possible. A start was to be made with the "reform of the head" before the council undertook to do so, thereby entering upon a path which at Basle had led to a schism.

Religious Colloquy Instead of a Council

With the Pope's silent consent, not by his commission, the Emperor now made yet another attempt to come to terms with the Protestants by means of a religious colloquy. The omens were more favorable than at any other time. The eirenic ideas of the aging Erasmus (d. 1536) had not failed to make an impression—a number of Erasmians sat in princely Chanceries or on bishops' thrones. Paul III sent to Ratisbon, in the capacity of legate, the man who was most sincerely in favor of an understanding, Cardinal Contarini. Once again the union was wrecked, not indeed because the compromise on justification (man is made righteous by a twofold righteousness, the righteousness of Christ and the righteousness that is communicated to him) which had been agreed upon, was rejected both in Rome and by Luther, but in the last resort by the divergent concept of the Church entertained by both parties. When the Protestants rejected the doctrine of transubstantiation in the Eucharist as defined by the fourth Lateran Council, Contarini declared that any further concession would only lead to a sham accord (*concordia palliata*).

From the birds'-eye point of view of history it is easy to say that at Ratisbon the impossible had been attempted. But was not the unity of the Church as Christ willed, so great a good that even the impossible must needs be tried?

First Convocation to Trent (1542)

Immdiately after the failure of the Ratisbon negotiations for reunion, Paul III, seriously disquieted by the infiltration of Protestantism into Italy, took up once more the plan for a council. His nuncio, Morone, the Curia's ablest diplomatist, came to an agreement with the Estates of the Empire at Speyer on the locality of the assembly. The choice of Trent, which belonged to the Empire but was of easy access from Italy and a predominantly Italian city, was only reluctantly accepted by the Pope. The lord of the city was the Prince-Bishop, Cardinal Christopher Madruzzo. Albrecht Dürer has left us a sketch of the city in his record of his Italian tour. Dominated by the imposing mass of the bishop's castle which had been further enlarged by an additional wing in the Renaissance style, the city, which at this time counted rather less than six thousand inhabitants, could only with difficulty provide accommodations for over a hundred bishops and for the envoys of the powers and their suites. When the number of participants rose sharply in the course of the third period of the council, the problem of providing accommodation became acute.

This second conciliar convocation, the first Tridentine one, proved unsuccessful. A fortnight after the promulgation of the Bull of convocation (May 22, 1542) Francis I declared war against the Emperor. Once again the papal legates waited in vain for the arrival of the prelates. In the end the Pope and the Emperor agreed, at an encounter at Busseto, near Parma, in June 1543, to postpone the council. As the war went on Charles V, who needed the military assistance of the Protestants, saw himself forced, at the Diet of Speyer, in the summer of 1544, to make concessions to the latter which led to a state of great tension between Rome and the imperial court. In a warning Brief the Pope evoked the memory of the grievous conflicts between the Papacy and the Empire in the Middle Ages. By the time the Brief reached the Emperor, events had rendered it obsolete. The Peace of Crépy, in September 1544, cleared the way for the council. In a secret article Francis I had declared his acquiescence in the opening of the council at Trent and promised to have France represented. On November 19 the Pope rescinded the suspension of the council and convoked it for *Laetare* Sunday, (March 15, 1545), to Trent. In addition to this, in the late spring of 1545, Pope and Emperor agreed on joint action against the German Protestants. The first step was to break the military power of the League of Schmalkalden, after which the council would be held, with the participation of the Protestants. In this way it became an element of a great plan the aim of which was the elimination of the breach in the Church.

The War of Schmalkalden
and the Council of Trent (1545-47)

The time-table could not be kept. When the Emperor opened the campaign in July 1546, for which the Protestants' fresh refusal to attend the Council of Trent was the military pretext, he was already behind the original date, and by this time the council had already been at work for six months. It had been inaugurated on December 13, 1545, in the presence of no more than thirty-one bishops, most of them Italians. It was presided over by three papal legates, namely Cardinal Del Monte, who by reason of his seniority in rank, was the head of the assembly; the learned Cervini who, as the trusted friend of the Pope, was its heart, and the Englishman Pole, an exile on account of his refusal to sign the Act of royal supremacy.

A decision had been taken on January 22, 1546, to deal simultaneously with the two main tasks of the council which had been expressly mentioned in the Bull of convocation, namely the definition of Catholic dogma and the reform of the Church. In the fourth session, on April 4, a decision had been taken on a question of principle which was to determine the whole course of the proceedings. It was to the effect that the apostolic traditions must be accepted with the same reverence (*pari pietatis affectu*) as the Sacred Scriptures, the canon of which was fixed at the same time. In the same session the Latin translation of the Bible in general use, St. Jerome's Vulgate, was declared authentic, that is, adequate for dogmatic proofs. But it was by no means the Council's intention to render the study of the original Biblical tongues superfluous, still less to forbid it.

The council had also given itself a constitution, which departed considerably from that of the councils of the fifteenth century. The bishops, the generals of Orders and the representatives of the monastic congregations (but not their proxies, nor the representatives of ecclesiastical corporations, such as cathedral chapters or universities) were entitled to vote. The vote was to be personal, not by nations. Although the council was the "representation" of the whole Church even in the opinion of the legates, in virtue of its convocation, it refrained from heading its decrees with the formula *Ecclesiam universalem repraesentans,* as had been done at Constance and at Basle, in spite of proposals to that effect by the Spaniards and a few Italians. The order of business comprised three stages. The first stage consisted of the "congregations of theologians" not of episcopal rank. They discussed at length whatever problems were submitted to them; their duty was merely to provide information for the bishops. In these congregations some of the luminaries of contemporary theology were to be heard, men like the Dominican, Dominic Soto and the Franciscan, Alfonso de Castro. The second stage consisted of the general congregations of all the prelates entitled to vote. These congregations were at first held in the great hall of the legates' residence, the Palazzo Prato, and later on, as the number of participants increased, in the Renaissance church of Santa Maria Maggiore. In these assemblies every member gave his *votum* on the dogmatic subject, or the question of reform, as the case might be. This often led to lively debates. The formulation of the decrees was the work of commissions chosen by the council; sometimes it was done by the legates themselves, with the assistance of professional theologians. In the solemn sessions, which were held in the romanesque cathedral of St. Vigilius, the only business was the voting on the completed decrees. The liturgical ceremonial was substantially the same as that already used at Vienne. The duties of a secretary were carried out in all three periods of the council, by the diligent Angelo Massarelli, to whom we owe the carefully drawn up protocols now preserved in the Vatican Archives, as well as seven diaries. The right of making proposals, that is, the determination of the program of the discussions, belonged to the legates, but any member, even the representatives of the powers accredited to the council, were at liberty to offer suggestions to the leaders of the assembly.

In spite of the fact that the Emperor, through his envoy Francesco de Toledo, insisted on the discussion of dogma being held over, the legates, to prevent the assembly from crumbling away, pushed on the discussions without a pause. The fifth session, on June 17, 1546, accepted the decree on original sin which was aimed against the Pelagians as well as against the reformers' teaching on the survival of original sin even after Baptism. A reform decree gave the bishops the right to supervise preachers, even those of the exempt Orders. Discussion of the chief article, that of justification, had only just begun when the issue of the first engagements in the war of Schmalkalden put the continuance of the council at Trent in jeopardy.

It was learnt at Trent that the Protestant General Schärtlin had stormed the pass of Ehrenburg and was threatening the other Alpine passes. Panic broke out among the Italians who, as a matter of fact, had only unwillingly come to Trent, and it was with difficulty that the legates, with the help of Madruzzo, kept the assembly together. They did not dare make use of the authorization of transferring the council which they possessed, without previous consultation with the Pope, even though they groaned under the ceaseless pressure of the imperialists.

A Stormy General Congregation

The course of the general congregation of July 30 shows how sharp the shock of opinions was during

those exciting July days. The pre-arranged date for
the next session had been allowed to lapse. Would
it not be better to refrain altogether from fixing a new
date since owing to the course of the war everything
was in suspense? Del Monte was in favor of letting
the question of a date lapse although two days earlier
a small majority (29 against 25) had spoken in favor
of fixing a date. The leader of the Spaniards, Cardinal Pacheco, protested vehemently against so arbi-
trary a procedure. The legate appealed to the principle that votes must be weighed, not merely counted.
Thereupon, in a raised tone, Pacheco asked: "Is then
my vote not worth as much as that of the others?"
Madruzzo begged the legate to deal with the council
in a more courteous and Christian fashion; otherwise,
he added in a threatening tone, he would feel obliged
to use another kind of speech. At this Del Monte's
wrath flared up: "I am not conscious of having acted
in an unchristian manner. Am I, the president, to
be lectured? Change your tone and I will change
mine. There is no question here of the freedom of
speech, the question is whether or no we must bow to
veiled threats (by the imperialists). They may use
violence against me—they cannot frighten me." For
the president the two cardinals were at this moment
the embodiment of the imperial power which detained
him at Trent and restrained his freedom of action.

However, Madruzzo stuck to his right of speaking
his mind freely and of remonstrating even with the
president. The hot-blooded Pacheco, now thoroughly
roused, even went so far as to throw in his face the
accusation: "You treat us like lackeys." So violent
did the quarrel become that the Archbishop of Palermo, falling on his knees, with hands raised in
supplication and amid tears, begged the three cardinals to put an end to the shocking scene.

The president insisted that the majority in favor of

a fixed date was not a genuine majority because a number of the votes had conditions attached to them, so that they could not be counted simply as favorable ones. Moreover, his colleague, Cervini, with whom he shared the leadership of the council, was absent. He would make no concession.

For all that, at the conclusion of the meeting, Pacheco and Madruzzo asked his forgiveness, should they have offended him. Del Monte replied with a nod. Madruzzo, revolted by this treatment, now so far forgot himself as to remark: "You can interpret my words as you like—I am a nobleman." Mortally offended by this allusion to his humble origin, Del Monte replied: "Yes, I am not a nobleman, but I shall go to a place where no one will be able to play off his nobility against me." This was a threat of the *translatio* which the imperial party wished at all costs to prevent.

Justification — The Sacramental Concept

Rumors of an impending translation of the council into the interior of Italy had reached even Charles V. He ascribed responsibility for the step to Cardinal Cervini who was regarded as the Pope's trusted friend, which in fact he was. However, the plan for a translation was rendered unnecessary because before long the Emperor, whose army included papal soldiers, succeeded in stabilizing the military situation. The debate on justification was resumed in September. Special questions came up for discussion, such as the degree of certainty of grace and salvation and the problem of a twofold righteousness which had been broached at Ratisbon. Only the third, revised draft of the decree, to the formulation of which Cardinal Cervini and the general of the Augustinians, Seripando, had contributed greatly, was given practically unanimous approval by the council in the sixth session held on January 7, 1547. In sixteen doctrinal chapters the Catholic teaching on justification was expounded in a positive fashion, while thirty-three canons condemned the opposite errors. The two decisive points were these two statements: 1. The co-operation of the human will with divine grace, which precedes the entire process of justification, and which creates the possibility of human merit; 2. An inward sanctification of man (in opposition to a mere declaration of righteousness) through sanctifying grace. It has been said, not without reason, that the religious cleavage could have been prevented, or that it might have taken a different turn, if this decree on justification had been promulgated by the fifth Lateran Council.

By comparison with the practical unanimity with which the council delimited the Catholic doctrine of justification from the Protestant, strong differences of opinion between the Spanish and the imperial group on the one hand, and the Italian majority on the other, came to the surface as soon as the problem of reform was taken in hand. One of the most grievous injuries to the life of the Church was due to bishops and parish priests not performing the duties of their offices in person but leaving them to substitutes. As early as May 1546 the Spaniards had asked for a debate on the duty of residence. In the first days of July several prelates, among them one of the three French members of the council, had submitted to the legates several memoranda on the impediments of residence, that is, the whole aggregate of hindrances of episcopal activity from above and from below, from the Curia and from the State. The decree submitted in the sixth session, on the observance of the duty of residence, which imposed a penalty for an unjustified absence of six months, was only a "small solution." It ignored the grievances of the bishops which for the most part were fully justified. When the votes were counted it was found that out of sixty bishops' votes only twenty-eight were in favor of the decree without any qualifications. It was only at a later date, on February 25, and after a thorough examination of the votes that had been handed in, that it became possible to declare the decree to have been accepted, after a promise to the opposition that these grievances would be dealt with. Another reform decree of the seventh session held on March 5, was accepted in spite of the opposition of four Spaniards. It forbade, among other things, the holding of several bishoprics by one person, since that was precisely one of the causes of the neglect of the duty of residence. It also laid down the basic principles for new regulations for offices and ordinations with which it was intended to meet the needs of the pastoral ministry. In the same session unanimous approval was given to a decree on the sacraments in general (their septenary number and their objective efficacy through the external performance of the rite) and on the sacraments of Baptism and Confirmation in particular. The core of this decree is the doctrine that the sacraments effect grace in virtue of their administration (*ex opere operato*), and not solely through the faith in the divine promises.

By this time the effective strength of the council consisted of sixty-four bishops and seven generals of Orders. Work was progressing apace and there was no hint of impending catastrophe.

Translation to Bologna

On March 6, the Bishop of Capaccio, in the Kingdom of Naples, a man in his best years, died after a short illness. In the course of the next few days further cases of illness and death occurred. The conciliar physician Fracastoro, who in the previous year had published an epoch-making work on infectious diseases, rightly diagnosed the sickness as typhus, the carriers of which were in all probability the soldiers returning from the German battlefield. The imperialists refused to admit the existence of an epidemic, while the legates, and the majority of the council, judged this to be the right moment for leaving Trent and thereby freeing themselves from the power of the Emperor. In the eighth session, March 11, 1547, they decided to transfer the council to Bologna, the second city of the Papal States. A minority of fourteen bishops protested. "The translation," one of them observed, "endangers the return of the erring Germans as well as the peace and unity of the Church." The great plan which formed the basis of the joint enterprise of Pope and Emperor was: first war, then a council. The council had gone forward more rapidly than the war, but since the turn of the year 1546-47, the Emperor's victory could be foreseen. The army of the confederates of Schmalkalden, which during the latter part of the autumn had faced the imperial army in South Germany, was forced to retreat through lack of money. One town after another surrendered to the Emperor — Ulm, Frankfort, Augsburg, and many smaller ones. In the opinion of the Pope the war was decided and the requisite conditions for peace negotiations existed; he accordingly recalled his own contingent. But the Emperor wanted total victory. While the legates were leaving Trent for Bologna, the imperial army marched northwards, against the chief opponent, the Elector John Frederick of Saxony. The Elector was defeated and made a prisoner on April 24, 1547, near Mühlberg, on the Elbe.

But what of the council? By this time it was at Bologna, and no longer at Trent, on which Pope and

Emperor agreed. On April 21, a solemn session was held in the vast, Gothic church of San Petronio, with only thirty-six bishops. During the whole summer and autumn the council discussed the doctrine of the sacraments — the Eucharist, Penance, Extreme Unction, Matrimony, Holy Order, and material was collected for a reform of sacramental practice. However, no corresponding decrees were promulgated in the two sessions held at Bologna. Why this omission?

The translation to Bologna crossed the Emperor's great plan. He accordingly reinforced the minority, mostly Spaniards, that had remained at Trent, and demanded from the Pope the return of the council to that city. Paul III refused, on the ground that the decision to transfer the council was legitimate. Before any further negotiations the minority must obey and return to Bologna. Both sides shrank from a complete rupture, not to speak of a schism. When the Emperor lodged a solemn protest against the translation, on January 16 and 23, 1548, at Rome and Bologna respectively, the Pope consented to suspend the discussions at Bologna and even summoned representatives of the Bologna council, which in the meantime had been reinforced by a few Frenchmen, as well as representatives of the Tridentine minority, to Rome, to report. He, nevertheless, did not order the council to return to Trent.

At the armed Diet of Augsburg Charles V saw himself compelled to impose on the defeated Protestants a temporary solution—the so-called *Interim* of Augsburg, the doctrinal content of which, though Catholic, nevertheless made several concessions to the Protestants, such as Communion in both kinds and the marriage of priests. Side by side with this he published for the Catholics, a reform statute, for the execution of which the Pope, after some hesitation, sent two nuncios to Germany. It was not long before the

Interim turned out a failure, not only because it lacked the Church's approval, but above all because the remaining forces (priests, and especially preachers) were not equal to the task of bringing back to the Catholic religion territories that had been Protestant for a whole lifetime.

At Augsburg the Protestants, from sheer necessity, had agreed to send representatives to the Council of Trent—not to that of Bologna—though with qualifications which rendered their promises nugatory. These conditions were that the council must not be subject to the guidance of the Pope, and that the decrees already approved by Trent must be replaced by new ones. These reservations were still maintained by them in the year 1550, when the former president of the council, now Pope Julius III (1500-54), was prepared to do what his predecessor had declined to do, namely, to order the return of the council to Trent on May 1, 1551. The equivocal character of the Protestant promises which the Emperor deliberately ignored and of which the Pope was at first ignorant, was the cause of the failure of this first, and last, attempt to remove the division in the Church through a council, with the cooperation of the Germans.

Return to Trent (1551-52)

The council was opened at Trent, on the appointed date, May 1, 1551, by the Cardinal-legate Crescenzio, whose co-presidents were two bishops both of whom acquainted with the German situation, namely, Pighino and Lippomani. This was the twelfth session. However, discussions only started at the beginning of September, after the arrival of representatives of the German episcopate, above all that of the Archbishops of Mainz and Trier. In the course of the following months the number of German bishops rose to thirteen. The French bishops held aloof. King Henry II, lapsing into his father's attitude, refused to recognize the "convention" of Trent as a council.

Thanks to the preparatory work at Bologna, it became possible as early as October 11 to define, in the thirteenth session, the doctrine of the Eucharist, that is, the real presence of Christ in virtue of transubstantiation, hence also apart from its reception. The articles on the administration of the Eucharist in both kinds (the "lay chalice") were postponed for the time being. The debate on Penance and the anointing of the sick was likewise brought to a relatively rapid conclusion. In nine doctrinal chapters and fifteen canons relating to Penance the fourteenth session, held on November 25, defended the necessity of auricular confession, the judicial character of absolution and the obligation of satisfaction. The decree on Extreme Unction, which Luther had described as a mere ceremony, emphatically stated that it was a true sacrament.

The course of the debates on reform was less satisfactory. The proposals submitted by Crescenzio did not adequately meet the wishes of the episcopate and spared the existing practice of the Curia far too much. When Bishop Pseaume of Verdun, who has left a diary of the council, demanded the complete abolition of all monastic commendams (that is, the bestowal of monasteries on people who were not members of that particular Order), the legate rebuked him so sharply that the Archbishops of Cologne and Mainz complained bitterly to their Spanish colleagues. "Is this still a free council?" the Archbishop of Cologne asked the Bishop of Orense. The question was asked in a moment of not unnatural excitement and is no proof that the council was not free, but it is symptomatic of the prevailing state of tension.

The Protestants at Trent

Tension grew with the arrival at Trent of deputations from the German Protestants, but the representatives of Brandenburg, who were the first to arrive, accepted the decisions of the council on October 11. The Württembergers, who were the bearers of a specially drawn up profession of faith of their own, the *Confessio Virttembergica,* and the envoy of Strasbourg, the historian Johann Sleidan, maintained their standpoint and refused to make any concession on questions of principle. They avoided all direct contact with the conciliar legate and only conferred with him through the imperial envoys. Together with the envoys of the Elector Maurice of Saxony, who arrived on January 9, 1552, they demanded a more satisfactory safe-conduct for their personal security than the one that had been granted them. The treatment of John Hus at Constance had not been forgotten. The safe-conduct was handed to them on the next day, but their further demands, namely, the abolition of the bishops' oath of fidelity to the Pope, the Pope's subjection to the council as understood by the decrees of Constance, a fresh discussion of the dogmatic decrees already accepted, the council could not accede to without stultifying itself. Negotiations carried on behind the conciliar scene led to no result. The Emperor himself, who followed their progress closely from nearby Innsbruck, had no other advice to give to his envoys than that they should prevent the suspension of the council in any circumstances.

The council was already irretrievably bogged when disquieting reports from Germany forced the German bishops to return to their dioceses. The Elector Maurice of Saxony, who had allied himself with France in the summer of 1551, was preparing for war against the Emperor. Toward the end of March he struck the first blow and marched southwards by way of Augsburg. The Emperor was wholly unprepared and fled from Innsbruck. On April 28, 1552, the council, paralyzed as it was by the mortal illness of the legate, decreed its own suspension. The council of reunion had foundered.

When the Fathers of the council returned to their dioceses all that they left behind was in every respect nothing but a torso, for the council had neither authoritatively defined all controversial doctrines, nor had the problem of Church reform been satisfactorily resolved. Its decrees were without force of law since they lacked papal confirmation. The attempt made by Spain and Portugal to enforce them on their own authority prompted Julius III to embody the existing Tridentine reform decrees in a great reform Bull, with several complementary additions, but he died before its publication. Although the reform movement dominated the two conclaves of 1555, which elected first the former conciliar legate Cervini, who took the name of Marcellus II, and after his early death, Cardinal Carafa, who took the name of Paul IV, there was no intention to proceed with the Council of Trent. Paul IV saw it as a hazardous venture. A reform convention in Rome in 1556, which was to prepare the way for a fresh Lateran Council, had to be interrupted on account of the war with Spain. The initiative for a reopening of the Council of Trent came this time from France.

Calvinism in France

The first two periods of the Council of Trent were orientated toward Germany, the country where the divisions had begun. They were part of a great plan, ecclesiastical as well as political, for the restoration of the unity of the Church. It had been jointly concerted by the Emperor and the Pope, but they fell apart over its execution. The dogmatic discussions had taken account of Luther, Zwingli and other re-formers of the second rank, but scarcely any notice had been taken of Calvin whose chief work had long been there for all to see. The advance of Calvinism in Western Europe, above all in France, already dur-ing the reign of Henry II, and still more rapidly after the latter's death in 1559, thanks to the seesaw politics of the regent, Catherine de Medici, brought the defec-tion of "the Church's elder daughter" within the range of possibility. The council had not been closed in 1552—it had only been suspended. It now appeared to Paul IV's successor, Pius IV (1559-65) as the very instrument by which to prevent the defection of France and to complete the work of the council. Should it be a continuation of the first two periods, as Philip II of Spain insisted, or should it be a new council, as desired by France and the Emperor Ferdi-nand I?

The Bull of convocation of November 29, 1560, favored the former interpretation but did not exclude the latter. The council itself would decide. Germany adopted a negative attitude. The Protestant princes assembled at Naumburg gave a flat refusal to the nuncio, Commendone, on February 5, 1561. Abbot Martinengo who was to take the invitation to Eliza-beth I, was refused permission to land in England. The German bishops stayed away, lest they should be accused of disturbing the religious peace concluded at Augsburg in 1555. The remaining countries that had kept the Catholic faith promised to send bishops and envoys to the council.

Third Period (1562-63)

One hundred and thirteen prelates took part in the opening session on January 18, 1562. The number was, therefore, greater than it had been at any pre-vious period, so that Cardinal Seripando, now papal legate, could write to Rome that by comparison the opening session in 1545 had been more like a diocesan synod than an ecumenical council. It became necessary to transfer the general congregations to a more spacious hall, namely, the church of Santa Maria Maggiore, with the interior of which we are acquainted through the well-known engraving. Ercole Gonzaga acted as president. A son of Isabella d'Este, he was a prince in character and manner. He was supported by Seripando, by the well-known controversial theologian Hosius, and the canonist Simonetta who, as head of the *zelanti,* was soon to become a key-figure of the council, and by the Pope's nephew Hohenemps who, however, left Trent after a brief stay as he was in no way equal to the duties of a legate and did not even command the Latin tongue.

In order to by-pass the highly political question whether or not the council was a "continuation," the discussions began with a debate on a scheme for reform. However, its very first article, which dealt with the unresolved problem of the bishops' duty of residence, immediately conjured up the first conciliar crisis. The Spaniards, led by Archbishop Guerrero of Granada, together with a group of Italians, pressed for a declaration that the duty of residence was a divine ordinance (*de jure divino*); in this way they hoped to preclude the possibility of dispensations. The curialists saw in a declaration of this kind an attack on the primatial powers of the Pope. In the voting of April 20 they secured a bare majority (there were thirty-five *non placet* votes and thirty-four *appellantes,* that is, those who left the decision to the Pope), altogether sixty-seven *placet* votes. Thereupon the Pope sided with them and forbade a further discussion of this fundamental question while the legates Gonzaga and Seripando, who favored the idea of the *jus divinum* for the duty of residence, were made to feel his displeasure. For nearly two months the council was to mark time.

The crisis was only surmounted, at least partially, by the beginning of June. The legates met with no opposition worth mentioning when they once more took up the dogmatic discussions where they had been interrupted in 1551. In the twenty-first session, on July 16, they obtained the approval of the articles kept back at that time, namely, those on the use of the Eucharist (presence of Christ under both kinds) and in the twenty-second session, of September 17, that of the decree on the Sacrifice of the Mass. This decree stated that the Mass is a memorial as well as a representation of Christ's sacrifice on the cross, with which it is identical by reason of the identity of the victim and the sacrificing priest, Christ himself, but from which it differs by the manner of the offering which is a bloodless one. The demand for Communion in both kinds made by the Emperor and the Duke of Bavaria, was passed on to the Pope who granted it after the termination of the council.

The Great Crisis of the Council and How It Was Overcome

On November 13, 1563, Charles de Guise, Cardinal of Lorraine, made his entry into Trent at the head of thirteen French bishops. The attitude of the still youthful, energetic and highly-gifted cardinal greatly contributed to the sharpening of the second and severest crisis the council had to undergo. In the meantime the discussion of the decree on residence, which had been kept back in the spring, had been resumed and the debate on the Sacrament of Holy Orders had been initiated at the same time. Both these themes depended on the relation between the Pope's primatial powers and those of the bishops, which had not as yet been defined with dogmatic precision. To state the problem more accurately, the question was how

the institution of the episcopate by Christ could be
reconciled with the Pope's supremacy?

Considerable theological acumen and skill in formulating propositions were employed in preparing
a compromise that would be acceptable both to Rome
and to the *zelanti*, as well as to the French and Spanish opposition. However, every attempt at a solution
was wrecked by the intransigence of the opposing
parties. De Guise succeeded in persuading the Emperor Ferdinand I, now once more at Innsbruck, to
intervene in person. In a letter of May 3, 1563, the
monarch conjured the Pope not to resist a reform by
the council and to make it possible for that assembly
to proceed once more with its discussions by soften-
ing up the standpoint of the *zelanti*. There was reason to fear a similar intervention by Philip II.
Intervention by the secular power might well mean
the end of the council.

The state of extreme tension was expressed in mu-
tual recriminations and intrigues. A Frenchman
made the irreverent observation that the Holy Ghost
came to Trent in the baggage of the Roman courier.
It was true that as representatives of the Pope, the
legates were bound to abide by his directives; but it
was not true to suggest that the council had no will
of its own, that it was pliable to guidance from Rome.
No votes were bought with the financial assistance
which destitute bishops and theologians received
from the conciliar chest. Such assistance was necessary as the bishops of poor dioceses could not otherwise have maintained themselves in view of the
dearth that prevailed at Trent. But no conditions
were attached to it. It was given according to individual need, and in any case it was so slender that
the French Calvinist Languet made the sarcastic observation that the bishops sold their souls not more
dearly than the German mercenaries their military

service. It was also perfectly natural that in a period of crisis efforts would be made to soften up fronts and to attract members of the opposition to the side of the majority. Duke Cosimo of Florence, whose close relations with Pius IV were well known, pressed the bishops of his territory to put an end to their opposition. The answer of one of the two, that of the Bishop of Fiesole, is highly characteristic: "I gave my vote in accordance with my conscience," he said, "and I cannot alter it, even if my life were at stake on account of it. I am devoted to the Pope, and in all worldly matters I am prepared to obey you, my sovereign. But I value the salvation of my soul too highly to vote at the council against the dictates of my conscience."

During these weeks of greatest tension, death took a hand in the fate of the council. On March 2 and 17 respectively, the two senior legates, Cardinals Gonzaga and Seripando, died one after the other, worn out as they were by toil and anxiety. Pius IV replaced them by the ablest of his diplomatists and most trusted counsellor, Morone, and by the Venetian Navagero. Morone proved the saviour of the council. Assured, as he was, of the Pope's confidence, he paid no regard to the rival government of the *zelanti* and their leader, Simonetta, journeyed to Innsbruck to see and pacify the Emperor, and won over Cardinal de Guise for a compromise on the question of powers. In an autograph letter to Philip II the Pope pledged his word that he was in earnest with regard to Church reform. The twenty-third session of July 14, 1563, now rendered possible after an interruption of ten months, was the turning-point of the council. The assembly contented itself with rejecting the Protestant teaching on the Sacrament of Holy Order and with formulating the decree on residence more strictly, though without mentioning the *jus divinum*.

A decree prescribing the establishment of diocesan clerical seminaries at last called into being an institution for the training of the clergy which had been lacking up to this time. The assembly had realized that the appointment of theological lecturers—which was no more than the renewal of one of the Lateran canons—would not meet the demands of the age.

Morone's Great Scheme for Reform

At Vienne the bishops had submitted memorials in which they stated their demands for reform. At Constance the conciliar nations acted in like manner. At Trent these examples were followed by the bishops and to some extent even by the governments of such countries as were represented at the council. At the beginning of March, 1562, a group of Italians submitted a memorial; in April it was the turn of the Spaniards; on June 7, 1562, the Emperor's envoys presented the latter's *Reform libell* to the legates; on January 3, 1563, the French envoys submitted the petitions of the French bishops. All agreed that in the interest of an orderly pastoral ministry the authority of the bishops over the clergy of their dioceses, whether secular or regular, should be strengthened and that all hindrances to its exercise by exemptions and unjustifiable appeals to Rome and equally by the interference of the State, should be eliminated. Bearing in mind these national demands for a reform, some of them of a most incisive nature, as well as the more conservative views entertained in Rome, Morone, in the course of July, 1563, drew up a comprehensive scheme of reform consisting of forty-two articles. The scheme was discussed all through the autumn and after considerable revision it was accepted in the twenty-fourth and twenty-fifth sessions.

It laid down rules for the nomination and the proper duties of cardinals and bishops, the organization of diocesan synods, to be held annually, of provincial synods, to be held every three years, visitation of their dioceses by the bishops, reform of cathedral chapters, improvement in parishes and pastoral preaching. As for the reform of the religious Orders, the scheme restricted itself to certain general rules for the admission of candidates, the novitiate, the enclosure and other such matters. It is no exaggeration to say that these decrees of Cardinal Morone constitute the core of what is usually described as "the Tridentine reform." The salvation of souls was its decisive criterion.

The dogmatic discussions which went on side by side with those on reform, resulted in a decree on the sacramental character of matrimony, supplemented by the extremely important reform decree *Tametsi*. It was published in the twenty-fourth session on November 11. Clandestine marriages, that is, marriages contracted without witnesses, are not only illicit, they are also invalid. Henceforth only those marriages would be valid which were contracted before the parish priest and two or three witnesses. These marriages must be duly entered in the parish register. The final and twenty-fifth session, which lasted two days, December 3 and 4, promulgated additional decrees on Purgatory, Indulgences, the veneration of Saints, their relics and images. "It is a good and salutary thing to invoke the Saints; their relics must be honored by the faithful," so must the images of Christ and the Saints, "not because we believe them to possess a supernatural virtue," but by reason of the archetypes that they represent. Thus the decree on images was essentially a renewal of the definition of the seventh ecumenical council.

Conclusion and Execution

In spite of the obstinate resistance of the Spanish envoy, Count Luna, and certain bishops, Morone

hastened the end. He was concerned lest the council
should make still heavier inroads on the papal
finances. During the first period the annual cost had
been between 30,000 and 40,000 scudi, nearly a tenth
of the total papal income. In the third period the
cost was nearly three times that sum. The final session had originally been planned for mid-December
when, on December 1, a letter from the Pope's
nephew, Charles Borromeo, brought alarming news.
The Pope was ill, it said, the worst had to be expected. In order to preclude any controversy about
the council's right to elect a Pope, such as the one
that had occurred at Constance, though under entirely
different circumstances, Morone decided to advance
the date of the final session. This is why it occupied
two days, for all the earlier decrees were read once
more and submitted for approval. One hundred and
ninety-nine bishops, seven abbots and seven generals
of Orders gave their signatures. At the close of the
session Cardinal de Guise, at one time the leader of
the opposition, and now the spokesman of the council, led the acclamations to the reigning Pope and his
predecessors who had made it possible for the council to be held, to the Emperors Charles and Ferdinand,
and to all who had contributed to its success. With
the wish: "Go in peace," Morone dismissed the council. On January 28, 1564, the Pope confirmed its
decrees, without any exception or alternation, thereby
giving them force of law.

The Council of Trent was the answer of the highest
teaching authority in the Church to the Protestant
Reformation. It was likewise the fulfillment of the
ever rising demand for an internal renewal of the
Church. It was not a complete fulfillment, but it
contained as much as was attainable. It gave clear
norms to theologians and preachers. It drew doctrinal boundaries but did not divide where there was

as yet no division. The Protestant reformation was countered by Catholic reform. There was no simple return to the Middle Ages, but a modification of the ecclesiastical constitution and the pastoral ministry. But Trent no longer was the assembly of an undivided Christendom, as the fourth Lateran Council or even that of Constance had been. It was not like them suffused by the splendors of a Pope-King and an Emperor, but on the contrary, an outwardly modest act of self-examination and self-renewal. For that very reason, its influence has been all the more decisive.

Yet if the Papacy had not used all its authority to ensure the execution—and completion—of its decrees, thereby breathing life into them, the Council would scarcely have had the lasting effect on the Church and on history which it has had. On August 2, 1564, Pius IV created a congregation of cardinals for the authentic interpretation of the Tridentine decrees which exists to this day. The achievement of his nephew, Charles Borromeo, as Archbishop of Milan, made him the model of a Tridentine shepherd of souls. Pius IV's successor, Pius V, sent the official edition of the decrees of the council to all the bishops for their guidance. St. Peter Canisius brought them to Germany, and they reached even America and the Congo. In compliance with a commission of the council the Pope published the "Roman Catechism," a handy manual based on the Tridentine definitions of the doctrines of the faith, for the use of parish priests. In addition Pius V also published a revised Breviary and Missal, the reform of which had been begun, but not completed, at Trent. During the pontificate of Gregory XIII (1572-85) the nuncios were instructed to watch over the execution of the conciliar decrees in their respective territories. His successors Sixtus V and Clement VIII published a revised text of the Vulgate. The Popes also strove to obtain recognition of the council by the various States. In this they were successful in Spain, Poland and the Italian States, though not in France and Germany. However, "by reason of its duration, and still more on account of its range, its many-sided and timely activity, the depth and thoroughness of its decrees, the prudence of its constitutional, juridical and disciplinary enactments, the number and intellectual stature of participating scholars and, finally by reason of its after-effects, the Council of Trent has thrown all the other councils into the shade." [1]

In glaring contrast to this balanced judgment by a modern historian, the first historian of the Council of Trent, but one hostile to the Papacy, Paolo Sarpi (1619) described the Tridentine reform of the Church as a legend and the whole council as a cunning maneuver of the Popes hoping to recover their power. On the basis of better and ampler sources, Sarpi's book has been refuted, in a number of particular points, by the Jesuit Pallavicino (d. 1656) in his *History of the Council of Trent*, but even more strikingly by the indisputable fact that a whole epoch of the Church has been fashioned by this council. Three hundred years were to go by before another general council assembled. That council started at a point which Trent had left in abeyance—the doctrine of the Church.

---

[1] Sebastian Merkle, "Die weltgeschichtliche Bedeutung des Trienter Konzils" in *Vorträge der Generalversammlung der Görres-Gesellschaft, 1935.*

V
THE VATICAN COUNCIL

Like a cataract, the waves of the French Revolution and those of the secularizations that followed it, had swept over the seemingly ruinous edifice of the Catholic Church. They carried away everything that had linked the Church to the State and to the society of an absolutist era. German princely bishoprics and French court-bishops, thousand-year-old abbeys, such as Reichenau and Cluny, disappeared. Before that the Society of Jesus had been sacrificed to the absolutism of the Bourbon courts in the "Age of Enlightenment." When, after the fall of Napoleon, the flood had subsided, men were surprised to see the walls of the edifice standing firm. After a century of disregard, even of contempt on the part of the rationalists, the Church once more regained public respect. A defenseless Pope, Pius VII, had boldly faced the all-powerful dictator. De Maître and Chateaubriand discovered the greatness of the Papacy as a supranational institution while Lamennais, Montalembert and Görres perceived the opportunities which the magic word "liberty" gave to a Church hitherto fettered by State interference in her affairs. Once again the Church gave proof of her vitality—indestructible because of divine origin. Though impoverished and still hampered both within and without by the relics

143

of past political and ecclesiastical notions, she went
forward into the new age, the industrial era, the age
of the common man, by slow steps, not without opposition, with many a set-back—yet nothing could stop
her progress.

The "Syllabus" of Pius IX

Pius IX entered upon his pontificate on June 16,
1846, with a reputation of being a "liberal," that is a
pontiff capable of approaching the new tasks of the
Church with an open mind. As a result of the revolution of 1848, the Catholics of Prussia and the Aus-
tro-Hungarian Empire had gained freedom of movement. The result was a rapid development of the life
of the Church in those countries, but for the Pope it
proved a grievous disappointment. In order to escape
from the revolution he was forced to flee from Rome.
French troops prepared the way for his return. He
became profoundly convinced that a barrier must be
erected to prevent the irruption of modern philosophical and political ideas into the very heart of the
Church, and took up a suggestion of Archbishop
Pecci of Perugia, the future Leo XIII, to issue a list
of contemporary errors. As early as 1851-52 the
Viennese nuncio submitted to Archbishop Geissel of
Cologne a *Syllabus* of erroneous propositions, with
the request to have it examined by his theologians.
However, the compilation, which it was originally
intended to publish simultaneously with the definition
of the Immaculate Conception (1854), was not ready
by that date. Cardinal Fornari, who was charged
with the task, had not yet completed his work. A
pastoral instruction of Bishop Gerbert of Perpignan,
published in 1860, in which eighty-five errors were
condemned, was eventually used as a basis for the
contemplated *Syllabus* which was to be drawn up by
a commission of cardinals under the presidency of

Cardinal Caterini. The errors were summed up in sixty-one propositions. After yet another examination by an enlarged commission, it was sent on December 8, 1864, to all the bishops together with an encyclical —*Quanta cura*.

The *Syllabus* condemned both philosophical systems, such as rationalism and pantheism, and social systems, such as communism, errors on moral questions, especially on marriage, but above all errors about the Church and her relation to the State. The *Syllabus* was almost everywhere regarded as the Catholic Church's challenge to modern civilization and for that reason it was subjected to most violent attacks—in France its publication was actually forbidden. The *Syllabus* was, of course, a defensive measure. Once again the Church discharged her most essential task—the preservation of the treasure of the faith, by checking the uninhibited belief in progress and the exaggerated expectations of a generation that regarded itself as striding forward toward a perfect world. Very few of those outside the Church understood the prophetic words of Heinrich, a theologian of Mainz, spoken at the *Katholikentag* in 1865: "Tonic medicines are often bitter . . . only when the nineteenth century is no more than a memory will mankind understand how salutary and necessary that medicine was."

Announcement of an Ecumenical Council

Two days before the publication of the *Syllabus*, on December 6, 1864, the Pope detained the cardinals at the conclusion of a session of the Congregation of Rites. He then laid before them his plan "to remedy by an extraordinary means, that is by means of a council, the extraordinary distress of the Church." He thereupon requested the twenty-one cardinals then in residence in Rome, on whom he enjoined the

strictest secrecy, to let him have their opinion on the
expediency of an ecumenical council. The majority
expressed themselves in favor of such an assembly,
two opposed it, while six others expressed some misgivings. The most fully worked out memorandum
was submitted by the German Cardinal Reisach, a
member of the Curia. The cardinal based the necessity of a council on the fact that the last council, that
of Trent, had not expressly refuted the fundamental
error of the reformers, namely, their denial of the
hierarchical structure of the Church and her authority to teach unerringly. This omission had created
some uncertainty even within the Church herself. As
a matter of fact the four Gallican Articles, drawn up
for the Assembly of the French clergy in 1682, actually approved of the decree *Sacrosancta* of Constance. They likewise asserted that the dogmatic definitions of the Pope were only infallible if they
received the assent of the Church. In Germany the
Auxiliary Bishop of Trier, Hontheim, writing under
the pseudonym of Febronius, had maintained, in his
work entitled "On the State of the Church" (1763)
that in point of fact the Pope possessed no higher
power than the bishops and that his primacy was a
primacy of honor. Though revolution and seculari-
zation had rendered the exponents of these ideas
powerless, the ideas themselves were not fully overcome and refuted. The problem of the Church, the
object of recurrent discussions and controversies ever
since the days of Boniface VIII and Marsilius of
Padua, remained unresolved.

On March 9, 1865, the commission of five cardinals
appointed by the Pope for the preparation of the
council, held its first meeting at the residence of the
Cardinal Vicar, Patrizi. The secretary, Archbishop
Gianelli, mentioned a further motive for the convocation—the fact, namely, that no ecumenical council

had been held for three hundred years. So long an interval was without precedent in the history of the Church.

At the end of April, 1865, the Pope took a further step when he asked thirty-six bishops for their opinion on the plan: eleven from Italy, nine from France, seven from Spain, seven from Austria, Hungary and Germany jointly, and one each from Belgium and England. Among those whose opinion was sought were the Archbishop of Westminster, Cardinal Manning, and Bishop Dupanloup of Orleans. They were later to become bitter opponents. The bishops' replies substantially confirmed the arguments of the cardinals whose opinions had been sought in the first instance. They agreed on the fact that the spiritual confusion in which the world found itself cried for a clear statement both of the great Christian principles and of the authority of the Church. Eight memoranda favored the definition of papal infallibility.

So far no definite step had been taken. Two years went by before the Pope had cleared every objection out of the way. His closest collaborator, Cardinal Antonelli, was not enamored of the project of a council. He feared political complications and sought to dissuade the Pope. It was Dupanloup who now encouraged the Pontiff when he wrote: "My conviction is that the forthcoming council in Rome will present to the whole world the imposing spectacle of five or six hundred bishops, gathered from all points of the compass, and firmly united in one faith on all the great questions which interest mankind."

Convocation to the Vatican

A favorable occasion for lifting the veil of secrecy and for making a public announcement of the council, presented itself in June, 1867, when nearly 500 bishops from every part of the world came to Rome for the eighteenth centenary of the martyrdom of the Princes of the Apostles. In an allocution, on June 26, the Pope revealed to these prelates his plan "to hold a holy, ecumenical and general council of all the bishops of the Catholic world. Its object would be, by means of joint discussions and united efforts, to discover with God's help the necessary remedies against the many evils which oppress the Church." On July 1, in an address drawn up by the Archbishop of Kalocsa, the bishops then in Rome affirmed their solidarity with the Pope, affirming at the same time their adhesion to the Florentine decree of union, though without pronouncing the word "infallibility."

A year later, on June 29, 1868, the carefully worded Bull of convocation *Aeterni Patris* was published. The date of the opening was fixed for December 8, 1869, and the sessions were to be held in the Basilica of St. Peter in Rome. The Bull was addressed to all bishops, including titular bishops, the presidents of the monastic congregations, and the generals of Orders, thus determining the circle of members entitled to a vote as it had been at Trent. By a Brief of September 8, 1868, in accordance with the precedent established by the Councils of Lyons and Florence, which had been held for the purpose of bringing about their reunion with Rome, the Pope called upon the non-uniate Eastern Churches to participate in the council. However, the Patriarch of Constantinople returned the Brief unopened, with the remark that he was already acquainted with its contents (the text had got prematurely into the hands of the press). There was nothing to be hoped for from the participation of the Eastern bishops, because the Brief did not pay "due respect to Apostolic equality and brotherhood." The same line was taken by the non-uniate Patriarchs of the Armenians, the Jacobites and the Copts. The Anglican bishops and the Jansenists were not invited. On the other hand, on September 13, 1868, the Pope made a public appeal "to all Protestants and non-Catholics," pressing them to return to the one fold of Christ. The reaction of the Protestant public was definitely much more negative than that of the orientals. The Protestant High Consistory in Berlin rejected the Pope's letter "as an unjustified interference in our Church." On May 31, 1869, the delegates of the Association of liberal Protestants sent out a protest from Worms "from the foot of Luther's monument," against every kind of hierarchical and priestly tutelage, against every form of violence to the spirit and oppression of the conscience." Further refusals to concur came from Switzerland, France, Holland and North America. It was, therefore, clear from the beginning that this would not be a council of reunion.

Preparatory Work and Order of Procedure

At the Council of Trent prolonged delays, which were not without danger, were caused by the fact that the settlement of the order of procedure and the preliminary study of the subject-matter of the discussions had been left to the council itself. In order to avoid a repetition of this kind of inconvenience, the commission of cardinals charged with the general direction of business, decided to form five subsidiary commissions to prepare the material for the council: 1. The commission *De Fide*, or dogma, presided over by Cardinal Bilio, with twenty-four members. 2. The commission for ecclesiastical discipline, under Cardinal Caterini, the prefect of the Congregation of the Council, with nineteen members. 3. The commission for the religious Orders under Cardinal Bizzarri, with twelve members. 4. The commission for the Eastern Churches and the Missions, presided over by Cardinal Barnabò, with seventeen members. 5. The commission for ecclesiastico-political questions under Cardinal Reisach, with twenty-six members.

All these commissions, even the directing ones, called for the assistance of foreign in addition to Roman experts. Accordingly from Germany came Professors Hettinger and Hergenröther of Würzburg, and Bishop Hefele of Tübingen; not, however, the acknowledged leader of the school of historical theology in Germany, Professor Ignaz Döllinger of Munich. It was said that the Pope had been told that Döllinger would not accept an invitation; but the real reason for his not being considered was that he had made himself unpopular by his lectures on the temporal power of the Pope. France was represented by Charles Gay, a Canon of Poitiers, who was to play an important part in the formulation of the dogmatic constitutions, and when Newman begged to be excused, the English bishops sent the President of St. Edmund's College, Dr. Weathers, in his place, while from Spain came Professor Labrador of Cadiz.

The subsidiary commissions entered upon their task as early as 1868. Acting on the proposals sent in by the bishops, either collectively or singly, and by the superiors of religious Orders, they prepared material (*schemata*) for each particular subject of discussion. The main achievement, however, of this intensive preparation was an order of procedure in the work of the council which was published on November 27, 1869, immediately before the opening. It had been elaborated under the direction and with the cooperation of Bishop Hefele. The right of proposing subjects for discussion was reserved to the Pope as the head of the council. For the formulation of the decrees four permanent commissions, each of twenty-four members, were to be elected by the council. They were to work under the presidency of one of the five presidents, namely, Reisach, De Lucca,

Bizzarri, Bilio, and Capalti. The *schemata* prepared by the subsidiary commissions were to be passed on to them. A committee (*de propositis*) appointed by the Pope would examine the proposals submitted by the bishops. A plan was worked out for the seating of the council in the general congregations and the solemn sessions. On April 27, 1869, the Bishop of St. Pölten, Fessler, had been named secretary of the council.

The Vatican Council was incomparably better prepared to begin its task than any of those that preceded it. Incomparably greater also was the intense interest with which world opinion viewed this assembly. For the first time also in the history of the councils the world could be informed of all that happened by means of the press and the telegraph.

The Article in the *Civiltà Cattolica* and Public Opinion in Europe

In the Bull of convocation of the Council of Trent, the Emperor, the King of France and all Christian princes were invited to appear at the council, either in person, or to have themselves represented. There was no similar invitation in the Bull of convocation of the Vatican Council; the Catholic princes alone were requested, in general terms, to promote the success of the council. The motive of this change of attitude toward the State is easily perceived: it was to forestall any meddling on its part with the internal affairs of the council. The "orators" whom one sees in pictures of the Council of Trent, were absent from the stage of the Vatican assembly. It was of course impossible to secure complete disinterestedness on the part of the Powers—it was not even intended, but in the spring of 1869 it could be seen that contrary to all expectations, the Vatican Council would become the concern of high politics.

On February 6, the semi-official fortnightly review of the Jesuits, *Civiltà Cattolica,* carried an article "From a Paris Correspondent." It reported that in France there were expectations that the council would define the doctrinal points contained in the *Syllabus,* and above all the doctrine of papal infallibility, by acclamation. The article, which consisted of extracts from addresses sent in by members of the French clergy and put together in the nunciature, gave expression to opinions similar to those advocated by the editor of *L'Univers,* Louis Veuillot. Veuillot, who was one of the leaders of the French Catholic *intégristes,* did not expect anything from conciliar debates conducted on traditional lines. The outpouring of the Holy Spirit on the first Pentecost, he wrote, had not been preceded by any discussions.

The article had an explosive effect and the expectation of what was likely to happen caused much excitement. The German Church historian Döllinger published a series of five articles in the Augsburg *Allgemeine Zeitung* entitled "Der Papst und das Konzil." He used the pen-name "Janus." These articles not only refuted, on historical grounds, the undoubtedly exaggerated conception of papal infallibility advocated by Louis Veuillot and Dr. Ward and their followers, but they also attacked papal authority itself with a sharpness unknown since the days of Sarpi. In July the articles appeared in book form. Their impact upon public opinion in Germany was hardly softened by refutations such as Hergenröther's *Anti-Janus.* They even occasioned a diplomatic intervention.

In a circular dated April 9, 1869, the Bavarian Prime Minister, Prince Hohenlohe, warned governments of the various States against the consequences that might ensue for the State from the definition of papal infallibility. But there was no collective action of the Powers, such as he aimed at, because the leading statesmen of Prussia and Austria, Bismarck and Beust, adopted a waiting policy and declined to appoint envoys to the council. In point of fact this had not been anticipated by ecclesiastical authority. "The whole question of the participation of the authorities of the State in the council" Bismarck wrote on May 26 to his Roman envoy, Count Arnim, "rests on a basis which is wholly foreign, one that no longer exists for us, for it depends on a relation between Church and State that belongs to the past and is now completely changed." Bismarck was evidently thinking of the Council of Trent; his observation was undoubtedly correct. The French Government, whose troops had guaranteed the existence of the Papal States since 1849, insisted on the French Emperor's right to be represented at the council. The claim was made in a speech by the Prime Minister, Ollivier, on July 10, 1869, but to the Pope's intense relief, Napoleon III refrained from the nomination of a conciliar envoy although Maret, the Dean of the Sorbonne, pressed him to do so, in order, as he said, "to frustrate projects that would be disastrous for Church and State alike."

In a voluminous work entitled *On the Ecumenical Council and the Religious Peace* (1868), and in a defense of the same work, entitled *The Pope and the Bishops* (1869), Maret had upheld a moderate Gallican conception of the Church: "Neither the Papacy nor the episcopate, but the Papacy *and* the episcopate, are the depositaries of infallibility." Thereafter Veuillot treated Maret as if he had been guilty of heresy. Day by day Veuillot's journal carried lists of names supporting his conception of infallibility. A middle party, headed by Archbishop Darboy of Paris and Bishop Dupanloup, held that the definition of papal infallibility was not opportune. There was no need to define infallibility, Dupanloup wrote in *Observations*; the doctrine that the Church is infallible has been found sufficient during the whole of eighteen centuries. Trent has issued no definition, precisely in order to prevent disunion among the bishops. Grave difficulties, both theological and historical, militated against it. It would set up a barrier against the Eastern Churches and the Protestants and give rise to conflicts within the State.

At their meeting at Fulda, under the presidency of the Archbishop of Cologne, Melchers, the majority of the German bishops declared the definition of papal infallibility inopportune and they wrote to the Pope in that sense in a joint letter dated September 4. In a joint pastoral letter they also sought to allay public excitement: "The council," they wrote, "will not set up new doctrines, differing from those that faith and conscience have engraved upon your hearts." On the other hand Archbishops Dechamps of Malines and Manning of Westminster were open and decided champions of the definition. The leaders of the French infallibilists, as they were called, were Cardinal Donnet of Bordeaux and Bishop Edouard Pie of Poitiers.

The Opening

"Magnificent beyond description," Bishop Ullathorne wrote after the opening session on December 8, 1869. The right transept of the Basilica of St. Peter had been transformed into a conciliar *aula*. The bishops' seats rose in eight tiers on either side. Wearing silver-cloth copes and white mitres, 642 prelates entitled to a vote took their places. The officials of the council—its bureau—had their places in the middle space, on the floor of the hall. On either side, above the bishops' benches, there were tribunes for the theologians and for distinguished guests. At one end of the hall, and visible to all, there was an altar. The volume of the Bible rested on a special throne. "Such an assemblage of prelates, whether you consider numbers, or the character of their training and breadth of experience, was never witnessed in the world before," he reported on the following day.[1] Ullathorne was right when he added: "Never did a council begin in better and holier dispositions." His evidence were the strong faith of the prelates and their loyalty to the Church. Some qualification of Ullathorne's remarks is, nevertheless, necessary since he seems to have forgotten the divergent views of some of the Fathers in the controversy about infallibility before the council.

The Vatican Council surpassed all previous councils by the number of the bishops who attended it. Out of a total of some 1,050 Catholic bishops, 774 took part. They came from all five continents; 146 from the English-speaking nations. Thirty came from Central and South America, that is, from parts practically unrepresented at Trent. Forty came from Germany and Austria-Hungary. There were fifty members of the Eastern Churches. Russia alone refused permission to her Catholic bishops to leave the country. The ecumenical character of the council was more evident than on any previous occasion of the same kind.

The First Dogmatic Decree

The *schema, De Fide,* of which an official printed copy was distributed on December 10, and which linked up with the *Syllabus,* was subjected to sharp criticism by Cardinal Rauscher of Vienna in the very first of the six general congregations in which it was debated. He complained that it did not take sufficiently into account the actual needs of the time and

[1] *The Vatican Council,* Vol. I, pp. 159, 162.

that "it smelt too much of the lecture-room." Arch-bishop Connolly of Halifax remarked ironically: "If the Tridentine theologians could read this *schema* they would rise from their graves and say 'See how we did this kind of thing!'" Bishop Verot of Savan-nah in Georgia, U. S. A., expressed the opinion that instead of refuting the obscure errors of German idealists it would be much more to the point to con-demn the notion that Negroes have no souls. Scarcely five years had elapsed since the War of Secession.

The *schema* was not "buried," as had been de-manded in the debate, but during the months of January and in the course of February, 1870, it was given a completely new and more compact formula-tion by a subsidiary commission in which Bishop Martin of Paderborn and the theologians Gay and Kleutgen had done valuable work. In this new form it was submitted to the members of the council on March 1, given a second reading, and discussed from March 22 to April 6. The very first day of the de-bate witnessed a "scene"—the only one during the whole of the council.

Bishop Strossmayer of Diakovár, in Bosnia, one of the best speakers of the council but also one of the most temperamental, pointed out that the *schema* traced contemporary philosophical errors, such as Rationalism and Pantheism back to Protestantism, although they had existed long before the religious cleavage and had been fought by Protestants also, as was shown by Guizot's book against Renan's *Life of Jesus*. But when he went on to say: "The Protestants err on a question of fact, but they err in good faith," the assembly became restless. The president, Capalti, interrupted the speaker by observing that it was not a question of Protestants as individual persons, but of Protestantism as a doctrinal system. To this Strossmayer rejoined: "I thank your Eminence for this information, but your argument does not convince me that all these errors must be laid at the door of the Protestants." There were many Catholics, he added, who wished with all their hearts that the decree should contain nothing that might prove an obstacle to God's grace, which is also at work among the Protestants. Capalti denied that the text of the *schema* contained anything of such a nature. But when Strossmayer proceeded to suggest that he felt oppressed in his conscience by the principle of a majority vote, a storm of indignant protests arose and he stepped down from the speakers' rostrum.

Scenes of this kind occur also in modern parliaments without necessarily leading to the conclusion that freedom of speech is suppressed. Strossmayer's criticism was not without justification. When it was repeated on the very next day by the Bishop of Châlons, that prelate was not interrupted. The result was that a whole series of formulations to which exception had been taken, though by no means all of them, were taken out of the draft. Most of the three hundred corrections that were suggested were on points of style. On April 24, 1870, in the third session of the council, the first dogmatic decree, on a question of faith, divided into four chapters and supplemented by eighteen canons, was accepted by 667 votes. The four chapters treat of 1. the existence of a personal God and the possibility for man to know him; 2. the necessity of a divine revelation; 3. the nature of faith; 4. the relation between faith and knowledge.

Debates on Pastoral Problems

During the interval between the two debates on the decree *De Fide*, that is, from January 8 to February 22, the council concerned itself with questions of ecclesiastical discipline and the pastoral ministry on which a vast number of suggestions, occupying 300 folio columns, had been sent in from every part of the world. Since pastoral conditions vary from one country to another, it is easy to understand why the *schemata* drawn up by the preparatory commission did not invariably meet with the approval of the bishops but were often subjected to unsparing criticism. Archbishop Darboy complained that only the duties of the bishops and their vicars general were mentioned but not their prerogatives. He thought that the drafts failed to state the problems clearly and in a manner corresponding to the actual situation. Their authors seemed to him like men viewing the world from the back of a cave. Cardinals Schwarzenberg of Prague and Matthieu of Besançon complained of the absence, in the draft, of any prescriptions for the cardinals and the officials of the Curia. The most interesting and critical speech was made by Bishop Strossmayer.

In the *schema* on the conduct of the clergy reference was made to the Breviary. Bishop Verot of Savannah expressed a wish for a better choice of readings from the homilies of the Fathers of the Church: "I confess that I cannot read without distraction St. Augustine's explanation of the thirty-eight years the sick man at the Pool of Bethsaida had been in his infirmity." Thereupon the president called out: "The Right Reverend speaker should speak with greater reverence of the holy Fathers." Verot replied: "Your Eminence, I wish to speak with all reverence of the holy Fathers, but at times even Homer nods—*quandoque bonus dormitat Homerus*. Apocryphal stories and preposterous homilies, such as that in which St. Gregory asserts that the end of the world is at hand, should be eliminated." The president: "The subject-matter of the debate is clerical life—the speaker has given sufficient expression to his wish for a reform of the Breviary."

It was not easy to get speakers to keep to the point when there were such inexhaustible matters to be discussed. The debate from February 8 to 12, on the introduction of a uniform catechism for the whole Church, brought to light widely divergent opinions on the practical value of the catechisms of St. Robert Bellarmine and St. Peter Canisius. These *schemata* were recast and debated a second time in May, but neither of them reached the stage of publication. It was probably realized that in this sphere uniformity was neither attainable nor desirable. As for the stock of valuable material which had accumulated on the subjects of the religious Orders, Eastern Rites, and the missions—they were never discussed at all; but together with the material for ecclesiastical discipline, they proved most useful when, decades after the council, work was begun on the new code of Canon Law.

The Question of Infallibility Becomes Acute

Meanwhile the question of papal infallibility, which had excited and divided the minds of many previous to the council, came to dominate everything else. The opposing fronts had been formed already in December when the *deputatio De Fide*—that is, on questions regarding the Catholic faith, was constituted. Led by Cardinal Manning, who was seconded by Archbishop Dechamps of Malines and Bishops Senestrey of Ratisbon and Martin of Paderborn, the "infallibilists" had drawn up a list in which not a single name of a declared opponent of papal infallibility was to be found. The latter, most of them Frenchmen (as, for instance, Matthieu, Darboy and Dupanloup), Austrians and Hungarians (Schwarzenberg, Rauscher, Simor, Haynald), and Germans (Melchers, Hefele, Ketteler of Mainz), drew up an opposition list, but they made no headway. Encouraged by their success, the leaders of the infallibilists decided on December 23, to collect signatures for an address praying for the definition of papal infallibility. When the petition was presented to the Pope in the last days of January, 1870, it bore the signature of 380 prelates. The memorandum handed in by the opposition was signed by only 140.

The methods pursued by the infallibilists in their campaign had created so much mistrust in the minds of the minority, that they saw in the supplementary regulations for the mode of procedure published on February 22, an attempt to outvote them. Whatever may have been the motives of their authors, if we view the matter objectively it can hardly be denied that they greatly contributed to the shortening of the discussions. The necessity of such a measure had become evident. It included three important regulations. 1. Written proposals for the improvement of the text of the *schemata* may be submitted even before they come up for discussion. 2. Voting is to be by simply standing up, or by remaining seated, as the case may be. 3. A proposal for the closure of a debate made by ten Fathers of the Council must be considered by the assembly.

However, the fact remains that these supplementary regulations were an innovation. The order of procedure at the Council of Trent, which Massarelli set down in writing only at a later date, which, therefore, is not an official document, contained no such restriction of the oral debates. This document came into the hands of the minority through the Prefect of the Secret Vatican Archives. Five protests against the new regulations from members of the minority met with no response.

When these proceedings are viewed dispassionately from the distance created by the lapse of time, it may well be asked whether there was any other way by which the dragging course of the debate could be speeded up, and a result arrived at, when nearly 700 voters, bound by no discipline such as binds the members of a political party in a parliament, might have been allowed to speak without any restriction or curtailment. What justification was there for the claim raised by the minority, that in matters concerning the faith "a moral unanimity" of the council was required? How many votes in a contrary sense would be required to nullify such a unanimity? There was no standard by which such a situation could be judged.

Reaction in Europe

Although the subject-matter of the debate was kept secret, the divergences of opinion which had developed within the council could not remain hidden. Press reports fanned the flames. Louis Veuillot, who was actually in Rome, provided his paper *L'Univers,* with reports. *The Tablet,* published several supplements dealing with the council. Some of the reports by Mozley, *The Times* correspondent, were misleading, since he had to rely on second-hand information. Much better informed was the author of *Römische Briefe vom Konzil,* who wrote under the pseudonym of Quirinus. These letters appeared in the *Allgemeine Zeitung* of Augsburg. The subject-matter was provided by two of Döllinger's pupils, Lord Acton and Johann Friedrich, who were in close contact with the German Cardinal in Curia, Hohenlohe, and who used the Bavarian embassy in Rome as an intermediary for getting their reports through to Munich. Even more critical than these writings was the pamphlet which appeared in Paris in the month of May, under the title of *Ce qui se passe à Rome?*—What is going on at Rome?—against which the presidents felt it incumbent on them to make a public protest. On January 21, Döllinger himself made a violent attack on the conciliar majority's petition to the Pope for the definition of infallibility, with the following assertion: "From the beginning of the Church to this day no one has ever believed in the Pope's infallibility." Döllinger received a great number of messages expressing agreement with his opinion, but Scheeben, an eminent theologian, "with infinite sorrow" described the article as "a declaration of war against the council," for Döllinger had been one of the leading figures in German Catholicism. Döllinger's former pupil, Ketteler, though a keen member of the minority, now dissociated himself from his former master. The controversial writings of Dupanloup, Ketteler, Hefele, Dechamps and many other writers on the problem of infallibility, fill a whole library shelf. The interest of public opinion in Europe was concentrated on Rome.

In March it looked as if some of the powers were about to intervene, but in the end Gladstone, two of whose informants were Döllinger and Acton, nevertheless desisted from such a step. In France, Daru, the *ministre du culte* and a friend of Bishop Dupanloup, failed to win the prime minister, Ollivier, over to his side. On the other hand, on February 10 the Austrian chancellor, Beust, instructed the Austrian ambassador in Rome to warn Antonelli that the canons on the relation between Church and State, foreseen in the *schema* on the Church but not as yet debated, would open an abyss between Church and State. Antonelli was greatly perturbed by these incidents, so much so indeed that on March 25 he personally made representations to the Pope, pressing him to withdraw the projected definition of infallibility. However, Pope Pius IX answered him: "I shall go forward."

Debate on Papal Primacy and Infallibility

The text of the *schema, De Ecclesia Christi*—On the Church of Christ—which was the theme of all these controversies, had been distributed to the Fathers of the council on January 21. Chapters 1-10 contained the doctrine of the Church in general; chapters 11 and 12 treated of the Pope's primacy and chapters 13-15 of the relation of the Church to the secular power. On March 6, in compliance with the above-mentioned memorandum submitted by the infallibilists, an appendix on the Pope's infallibility was added to chapter 11. Tension kept rising because of a rumor that an attempt would be made to get the dogma of infallibility accepted by acclamation. The rumor proved to be false. The *schema* of the Church was discussed in accordance with the agreed method of procedure.

In March and April the written amendments were handed in and printed; they filled 346 folio columns. On the basis of these amendments chapters 11 and 12 were recast by the deputation *de Fide*. It was now divided into four chapters, the rest having been omitted, and was submitted to the council on May 9; May 13, witnessed the opening of the memorable debate.

From the start the problem of infallibility constituted the central point of the debate. Archbishop Dechamps, avoiding the exaggerations into which Veuillot, a layman, and the eager Manning had allowed themselves to be betrayed, explained that the infallibility of the Pope is neither personal, since it belongs to his office, nor absolute, because it has conditions attached to it. From the opposite side Hefele raised the historical difficulties which stood in the way of the definition, in particular the "Question of Honorius." Maret's speech on June 3, was also the last discourse against the definition. Thirty-nine speakers had been in favor of the definition, twenty-six had spoken against it, and there was a waiting list of yet another forty speakers. Thereupon the secretary of the council, Fessler, informed the assembly that 150 Fathers of the council had proposed the closure of the debate since it could not be expected that any new light would be thrown on the subject even if it continued. The proposal was accepted amid the protests of the minority.

The closure of the general debate was no muzzling of the minority, for a special debate on the text of each particular chapter was yet to come. For this debate 120 speakers had put down their names. In the general congregations between June 15 and July 4, thirty-five orators spoke in favor of infallibility, twenty-two against it. Actually it is inaccurate to use such an expression, for the opponents of the definition were by no means opponents of infallibility itself. The latter, as Cardinal Rauscher made perfectly clear, linked the Pope's infallibility to the advice and witness of the universal Church. They hailed with jubilation a canon proposed on June 18, by Archbishop Guidi of Bologna: "Whosoever says that when the Pope pronounces a dogmatic definition he acts arbitrarily (*ex arbitrio*) and independently of the Church, let him be anathema." Strossmayer embraced the speaker and both Dechamps and Darboy saw in his proposal a basis for a possible compromise.

It was for such a compromise that the middle party, headed by Archbishop Spalding of Baltimore, had been working since February. Among those who sympathized with its efforts were some influential members of the Curia as well as the General of the Jesuits, Father Beckx. The party also included Cardinal Bonnechose of Rouen, Archbishop Lavigerie of Algiers and Bishop Forcade of Nevers, as well as Bishop Ullathorne of Birmingham whose letters from the council, on account of their impartiality, must be reckoned among the best sources of information on these dramatic events. The middle party kept aloof from the extremists (Manning of the majority, Dupanloup of the minority) and strove for a formulation of the doctrine of infallibility which would be acceptable to everyone. Aubert wrote: "Though they played a modest and somewhat thankless role, it was not a useless one."

The Definition of Papal Primacy

Before we turn our attention to the issue of the struggle we must refer to the special debates on chapters 1-3 of the *schema* dated May 9, which lasted from June 6-14. Its subject-matter was the institution (chap. 1), the continuation (chap. 2) and the extent of papal primacy (chap. 3). The first two chapters created no serious difficulties because all were agreed on the interpretation of our Lord's words in Matthew 16:18 and John 21:15, as well as the devolution of St. Peter's primatial authority to his successors. All the more complex was the situation in regard to chapter 3. The relation between the primatial power and that of the bishops had been a matter for controversy ever since the councils of the fifteenth century. Differences of opinion on the subject came near wrecking the Council of Trent. In the *schema* now proposed the definition of the Florentine Council of reunion was taken up once more, but with an additional clause that clarified it. It was to the effect that the Pope's primatial authority is an ordinary, immediate episcopal authority over the whole Church and over every particular Church, but that this authority cannot deprive the bishops of ordinary and immediate authority in their respective dioceses. It was the merit of Cardinal Rauscher and Bishop Freppel of Angers, a former professor at the Sorbonne, that they rendered the parallel working of two authorities intelligible by means of a few verbal changes in the *schema*. The bishops' immediate responsibility to God was confirmed by the additional clause that, as the successors of the Apostles, they are "set up by the Holy Ghost" (Acts 20:28). On the other hand, on the initiative of Manning, who in this instance was backed by the Pope, the additional canon contained a formula to the effect that the Pope possesses the fullness of this power (*totam plenitudinem hujus supremae potestatis*).

Of the seventy-two amendments the deputation accepted only four which it embodied in the text. In this way the definition of primacy, from an historical point of view the most important of all, received its final form in the light of the report submitted on July 5, by Bishop Zinelli of Treviso. The two decisive passages stated: "We renew the definition of the ecumenical Council of Florence, in virtue of which all the faithful of Christ must believe that the Holy, Apostolic See and the Roman Pontiff possess the primacy over the whole world, and that the Roman Pontiff is the successor of Blessed Peter, Prince of the Apostles, and is the true Vicar of Christ and Head of the whole Church, the Father and Teacher of all Christians; and that full power was given to him in Blessed Peter, to feed, rule and govern the universal Church, by Jesus Christ our Lord, as is also written in the acts of the general councils and in the sacred canons." And a little further on the definition continued: "but so far is this power of the Supreme Pontiff from being prejudicial to the ordinary and immediate power of episcopal jurisdiction, by which bishops, who have been set by the Holy Ghost to succeed and hold the place of the Apostles, feed and govern, each his own flock, as true pastors, that this pastoral authority of theirs is really asserted, strength-

ened and protected by the supreme and universal
Pastor. . . ."

The Definition of Papal Infallibility

In the general congregation of July 11, Bishop
Gasser of Brixen, in a speech of four hours' duration,
gave a full and, as was generally acknowledged, im-
partial account of the work of the deputation on the
fourth chapter of the draft of the decree of papal
infallibility. No less than 144 amendments had had
to be considered. Two days later this chapter was
submitted to the vote of the council. This was the
critical moment. Four hundred and fifty-one Fathers
gave their *placet*, eighty-eight gave a *non placet*,
sixty-two gave a conditional vote (*placet juxta mo-
dum*). The amendments suggested by the third group
necessitated yet another debate in which the final text
of the decree of infallibility was established. The
decisive passage runs thus: "We teach and define . . .
that the Roman Pontiff, when he speaks *ex cathedra*,
that is, when in discharge of the office of Pastor and
Doctor of all Christians, by virtue of his supreme
apostolic authority, he defines a doctrine regarding
faith or morals to be held by the universal Church,
by the divine assistance promised to him in blessed
Peter, he is possessed of that infallibility with which
the divine Redeemer willed that his Church should
be endowed for defining doctrine regarding faith or
morals; and that, therefore, such definitions of the
Roman Pontiff are irreformable of themselves, and
not from the consent of the Church."

The last sentence of this text excluded the necessity
of the concurrence of the universal Church in the
dogmatic definitions of the Pope on which the minority had insisted. The draft was accepted by nearly
every one of the 552 Fathers who assisted in the
council's last general congregation on July 16. The

striking numerical difference between this and the preceeding vote leads one to enquire what became of the missing votes.

On July 15, a deputation of the minority, consisting of Archbishops Darboy of Paris, Simor of Gran, Scherr of Munich, Bishops Ginoulhiac of Grenoble and Ketteler of Mainz, made a last-hour intervention with the Pope. They implored him to facilitate the unanimous acceptance of the decree by deleting the formula concerning the fulness of power in the canon of chapter 3 and the words "but not with the consent of the Church" at the end of chapter 4, the later clause to be replaced by one to the effect that in an infallible dogmatic definition the Pope must take into account the witness of the local Churches. The Pope declined to make the proposed alterations—he would not interfere with the decisions of the council. Thereupon, at the instigation of Bishop Dupanloup, the minority, whose numbers had shrunk considerably, decided to boycott the solemn session and to leave the city. Fifty-five members of the minority justified their action in a joint letter to the Pope.

On Monday, July 18, in the fourth session of the council, the constitution *Pastor Aeternus* was accepted by 533 *placet* votes against two *non-placet* ones. (They were the votes of Bishop Fitzgerald of Little Rock and Bishop Riccio of Cajazzo). At the same time the prorogation of the council was likewise decided. A violent thunderstorm raged while the session was in progress. The lightening flashed and the thunder pealed for a whole hour and a half. "A more effective scene I never witnessed," wrote Mozley, *The Times* correspondent. When the result of the vote was taken up to the Pope the darkness was such that a taper had to be brought, to enable him to read the text: "We define, with the assent of the holy council, all that has been read and confirm it in virtue of apostolic authority."

Acceptance and Opposition

On the day after the session the Franco-German war broke out. Two months later, on September 20, Piedmontese troops occupied the city of Rome. Pope Pius IX had become "the Prisoner of the Vatican." For the time being there could be no question of the resumption of the council, but to this day it has not been formally closed. The two dogmatic decrees of the Vatican Council have the form of papal constitutions, on the model of the Lateran Councils, because they were accepted in the Pope's presence and immediately ratified by him. Catholic dogma is thereby defined in two spheres which are particularly relevant to modern times. The constitution *Dei Filius* of April 24, 1870, defined the frontiers of faith and knowledge, knowledge by faith and by reason, while the constitution *Pastor Aeternus* of July 18, 1870, expressed the extent of the Pope's primatial authority and his doctrinal infallibility. The latter definition filled, at least in part, the gap left by the Council of Trent. The doctrine of the Church as a whole, which Trent also had left undefined, but which was included in the original *schema* of the Vatican Council, did not come up for discussion. As we look back today we feel inclined to see a providential purpose at work —the "era of the Church" had not yet begun.

Unlike almost all previous councils, the Vatican Council promulgated no disciplinary decrees. However, the prudent work of four of the five preparatory commissions, and of the corresponding conciliar deputations, in which every sphere of the pastoral ministry was taken into consideration, was by no means wasted. Pius X's reform legislation as well as the authors of the new ecclesiastical code, the *Codex Juris Canonici*, are indebted to the material accumulated at that time.

Two days after the session Dupanloup wrote: "The

great affair has been decided against us. Therefore,
nothing, not a word that could be understood in a
bad sense!" Not one among the minority bishops
refused to submit. Most of them did so at once;
others, like Hefele and Haynald, needed time to become reconciled to the definition. Strossmayer was
the last to make his submission in December 1872.
However widely opinions may have diverged at the
council on particular subjects, the episcopate was
completely united in its attitude to the Catholic faith.
On their return to their dioceses the bishops met with
a jubilant welcome in every part of the Catholic
world. When Archbishop Spalding arrived at Baltimore on November 10, he was welcomed by a crowd
of 50,000 people, who escorted him to the cathedral
while the bells of all the Catholic churches were
pealing. There were similar scenes in England, Ireland and Belgium. In France also, where both before
and during the council controversy had run particularly high, no opposition was encountered. Montalembert, the friend of Dupanloup and Döllinger,
had died on March 13, 1870, before the definition
had been pronounced. A few days before his death
he had written prophetically: "Despite all appearances
I am firmly convinced that, after much bitterness and
many storms, this crisis will prove to have a whole-
some and purifying effect."

The conciliar decision had a less smooth passage
in the German-speaking countries. On August 30 the
German bishops declared in a joint pastoral letter:
"The infallible teaching authority of the Church has
decreed: the Holy Ghost has spoken through the
Vicar of Christ and through the episcopate united
with him; hence all of us, bishops, clergy and faithful, must receive with a firm faith these decisions as
divinely revealed truths." The overwhelming major-

ity obeyed, but a group of intellectuals refused to submit. Their leader was Döllinger.

On his return to Munich, Archbishop Scherr, in the course of his reception at the railway station, said to Döllinger: "Let us get to work." Döllinger replied: "For the old Church." The Archbishop: "There is only one Church." Döllinger: "They have created a new one."

On August 25, at a conference convened by Döllinger at Nuremberg, a group of professors and other intellectuals formally denied the ecumenical character of the Vatican Council and the freedom of its decisions. Döllinger himself, owing to his refusal to submit in spite of repeated exhortations by the Archbishop, was excommunicated on April 17, 1871. His adherents constituted themselves into the "Old Catholic Church" and on June 14, 1873, at Cologne, chose the former professor of theology at Breslau, Reinkens, for their bishop. Shortly afterwards Reinkens received episcopal consecration from the Jansenist Bishop of Deventer. The protection which the Prussian government extended to the Old Catholic clergy was one of the contributary causes of the Prussian *Kulturkampf*. Bavaria took a similar line. The minister for Church affairs (Kultusminister), Lutz, regarded the Vatican decrees as a danger to the State. Austria used them as a pretext for denouncing the concordat concluded with the Holy See in 1855, on the plea that the other party to the convention was now a different body. The Hungarian government dropped an attempt to prevent publication of the decrees after protests by the Primate, Archbishop Simor. Nowhere was publication of the decrees prevented.

They have become part of the faith of the Church. The irreparable cleavage between the Church and the modern civilized world, which many shrewd observers feared, did not occur. The Popes who followed Pius

IX, above all his immediate successor Leo XIII, have
exercised their ordinary teaching office by means of
encyclicals on a scale hardly equalled by any of their
predecessors. On the other hand, the occasions when
a solemn *ex cathedra* decision was issued have been
very rare, and these alone are the subject of the Vatican definition. The moral authority of the Papacy
has been on the increase ever since.

Retrospect and Prospect

A backward glance at the history of general councils may give rise to a variety of considerations in the
reader's mind. They will be very different in the case
of a Catholic or a Protestant, or in the case of a
member of the Orthodox Church, to say nothing of
the likely reaction of those who reject the Christian
religion. It is not our intention to co-ordinate these
reflections when, in retracing our steps in this conclusion, we emphasize one or the other observation.

First of all come the problems of geography and
communications. If the localities of the twenty general councils were linked, the connecting line would
be a vast loop leading from the cities situated on the
land-bridge between Europe and Asia (Nicaea, Constantinople, Ephesus and Chalcedon), to Rome, thence
to France and into the German-speaking territories,
to return finally to Rome by way of Ferrara, Florence
and Trent. Eight of the twenty general councils were
held in the East, the leader as it was in ancient times,
in speculative theology. The remaining twelve are
distributed among the three nations that constitute
the core of Western Christendom—Italy, France, and
Germany. No less than six councils have been held
in Rome. This shows both the dominant position
which the Papacy enjoyed and the significance of
these three nations for the internal development of
the Church.

The means of communication were substantially the same for nineteen out of twenty councils. Journeys were made on foot, on horseback or by sea. Prelates, in their capacity of dignitaries of the Empire, had at their disposal great high roads, with their official postal relays. These were no longer in existence in the Middle Ages, which explains the small number of bishops from Portugal, Ireland and Scandinavia at medieval councils. Moreover, besides the length of the journey, there was the cost of the journey which was prohibitive for men like the Irish bishop at the third Lateran Council, whose possessions consisted of three cows. There are accounts of some very lengthy conciliar journeys. Bartholomew of the Martyrs set out from his episcopal city, Braga, on March 24, 1561, and traveling via Spain and Southern France, reached Trent two months later on May 18. The journey by sea was no less exhausting or dangerous. One of the two ships which were to take the Byzantine envoys to the second Council of Lyons was wrecked near the southern point of the Peloponesus and only one passenger escaped with his life. Martin Pérez de Ayala recounts in his autobiography that on the return journey from the second period of the Council of Trent contrary winds and the danger of pirates detained him for the space of three weeks on the island of Ibiza. Those who participated in the Vatican Council were the first members of such an assembly to have at their command both the railway and steamships, with the result that it was better attended than any previous council.

If the history of the Church is compared to a tapestry into which her destinies are woven, the councils will be shown to be its ever recurring pattern, though never the same. We are presented with a picture of events in which at a first glance, the ephemeral rather than the permanent makes the stronger impression.

What changes of scene alone! Constantine the Great in the summer residence at Nicaea, in the midst of bishops who had lived through the great turning point of history, some of whom had actually endured persecution; two empresses, Pulcheria and Irene, as co-organizers and patronesses of the Council of Chalcedon and the second Council of Nicaea respectively; exulting crowds acclaiming Mary's title of Theotókos, which Cyril of Alexandria had caused to prevail; a Pope-King, Honorius III, in his cathedral church of the Lateran, surrounded by the spiritual dignitaries of the whole, as yet undivided, Christendom; Thaddeus of Suessa's groan, full of forebodings, as the candles were extinguished in the cathedral of Lyons at the excommunication of Frederick II; the vast crowd outside the Merchant's Hall at Constance, after a schism that had lasted thirty-nine years, shouting: "We have a Pope!"; the modest procession of bishops who, twenty-eight years after Luther had put up his theses at Wittenberg, moved to the cathedral to inaugurate the most hotly contested as well as the longest of all the councils. There is a constant change not merely of actors, but also of conciliar issues.

The oldest of these assemblies have this in common with the most recent one that they were purely episcopal councils. In between there is a widening of the circle of participants in favor of abbots—as a token of the significance of monasticism in the Christian West; of the representatives of ecclesiastical bodies, cathedral chapters and universities, and finally even in favor of the representatives of the secular power. In the councils of the central period of the Middle Ages not only the Church but Christendom, both ecclesiastical and lay, were represented. The attempt at Basle to turn the council into an ecclesiastical parliament was in vain.

Subjects of discussion also changed. Settling disputes on questions of doctrine by establishing the fundamental dogmas of the Christian religion was the occasion for the oldest councils and their noblest task. The canons, which constitute the residue of their legislative activity, were an addition of utmost importance for the Church's constitution, liturgy and pastoral office. For five centuries the collections of canons regulated the life of the Church, and the science of Canon Law has been built upon them since the eleventh century.

The councils of the central period of the Middle Ages were concerned with good order both in the Church and in the world. They issued regulations for the election of Popes and the distribution of offices, prescribed the truce of God and taxes for the crusades; they condemned heretics because they were considered to disturb the ecclesiastical and social order. From the end of the thirteenth century the reform of the Church, later on to be described as *reformatio in capite et membris* (in head and members) provided, and remained, the main theme of the councils up to the Council of Trent, which may be described simply as a reform council. It also drew the line of demarcation between Catholic and Protestant teaching. Papal schisms were the main preoccupation of the second and third Lateran Councils. Above all it was the first concern of the Council of Constance. Schisms between the Eastern and the Western Church engaged the eighth general council, against Photius, as well as that of the second Council of Lyons and that of Ferrara-Florence.

A change occurred in the mode of procedure. Very little is known of the course of the discussions at the first two councils or at those of the Lateran up to the time of Innocent III, because no protocols were kept. But when such reports do exist they tell of extremely lively discussions. The Middle Ages altered the character of the sessions. They became concluding acts of a juridical and liturgical nature, summaries of what had been discussed in the full assemblies, now called general congregations. From the fifteenth century the cnogregations constitute the core of conciliar activity, while side by side with them "deputations," either elected or named by the presidents, for the purpose of preparing the material of the discussions, acquire an ever increasing importance. At the Vatican Council the order of procedure was a subject of heated controversy.

Councils are ecclesiastical gatherings, but since the Church is the Church of the whole world, their history reflects the changes in the relationship between Church and State. They were increasingly linked with politics. For Constantine the Great it was a political act to convoke the Council of Nicaea. By means of the second Council of Constantinople Justinian hoped to attach Monophysitic Egypt again more closely to the empire. At the first Council of Lyons an emperor was deposed. At Vienne Philip the Fair pressed the proceedings against the Templars in the hope of restoring his financial situation. Francis I sabotaged the Council of Trent because he imagined that it would add to the power of Charles V. Even the Vatican Council occupied the attention of leading statesmen of the period, such as Bismarck and Gladstone, although the great powers had been deliberately ignored in the Bull of convocation.

It would, however, be a superficial reading of historical facts that regarded the political motives of those who convoked the councils, and the politics which were their by-products, as their chief function. On the other hand it would be no less misleading to overlook the permanent element amid the ever changing scene of the historical pageant.

One permanent element is the cooperation of head

and members of Christ's body in the profession of a common faith and in the solution of the tasks which Christ laid upon the Apostles and their successors by his apostolic and pastoral commission. "As the Father has sent me, so do I send you; go, teach all nations, baptizing them . . . and I am with you all days." These words of Christ are the justification of the claim of the bishops assembled in council to regulate the teaching and the discipline of the Church. Their consciousness that in the execution of their teaching duty they have the assistance of the Holy Spirit is as vivid as was that of the Apostles who concluded their conciliar decision with the words: "It has seemed good to the Holy Ghost and to us."

Yet the assistance of the Holy Ghost who, according to Catholic teaching, guarantees the decisions of a council to be free from error, does not dispense with the most strenuous efforts to arrive at the truth; on the contrary, it presupposes and demands such efforts. Truth is reached in any community by means of an exchange of opinions, by arguments for and against, that is, by means of an intellectual struggle. At the councils, as in any other place where men contend with one another for the truth, fallen human nature exacts its toll: the former, that is the struggle, is ordained by God, the latter he permits. Opinions may differ about the methods used by St. Cyril at Ephesus, or by Innocent IV at the second Council of Lyons, without the legality of the results of these two councils being called in question. The toll paid by human nature in the councils is the price which the visible Church has to pay for being in the midst of the human race.

Conciliar proposals are not the same thing as conciliar decisions. When certain Fathers of the Vatican Council pointed to the shortcomings of the disciplinary proposals, they were not actuated by negative

criticism but were obeying the dictates of their con-
sciences. Yet it was an obligation of conscience also
for the presidents to see the good order and the
progress of the discussions. There are "parties" at
a council and there is an "opposition," in fact it might
be said that a council without an opposition would
give rise to the suspicion that it was not a free council. The opposition of the Antiochenes at Ephesus or
that of the Alexandrians at Chalcedon made its own
contribution to the discovery of the truth. It was
due to the Augustinian party at Trent that the significance of faith and the righteousness of Christ were
so strongly emphasized in the decree on justification.
Even middle parties have their providential task. The
struggle over the *homoousios* was only brought to
a conclusion by the great Cappadocians. At the Vatican Council the middle party facilitated the clarifi-
cation and the determination of the limits of papal
infallibility.

Councils have to put up with eccentrics—men like
Bishop Martelli of Fiesole, the irrepressible champion
of episcopal prerogatives at Trent, and Bishop Strossmayer, the temperamental advocate of freedom of
speech at the Vatican Council. They even have to put
up with intrigues, such as those spun by Simonetta
and Manning, in the hope that in the end truth, and
nothing but the truth, would prevail. The fact that
some very human incidents occurred in a number of
councils cannot infringe their authority—they merely
demonstrate their freedom. An assembly of Yes-men
would be a distortion of a council of the Church.

The announcement of an ecumenical council by
Pope John XXIII, on January 25, 1959, has stultified
the prophecies of those who looked upon the definition of infallibility as an end to all councils. The
internal and external tightening of the constitution
of the Church which, after doing away with late

medieval fiscal centralism, began with the Council of Trent and reached its climax in the Vatican Council, differs fundamentally from every form of dictatorship. It does not, indeed it cannot suppress the personal responsibility of its members. That is why general councils fully justify their existence and function in the life of the Church.

We may go even further and affirm that our age requires a council for the assembly of which, as is evident, it offers particular facilities. Rapid means of information and communication have brought even the most distant parts of the world so close together that the convocation of a council is incomparably easier than at any period of the past. From a purely technical point of view, a council could be assembled within the space of one week. The transmission of invitations, which at one time required many months, even within the narrow confines of the Graeco-Roman world and the Christian West, could be accomplished within hours, even though the addresses are scattered over five continents.

Moreover, the world has become a unity to an unprecedented degree. Political conflagrations in Korea or Tibet concern the West as closely as those in Hungary or Berlin. Trade is abolishing the barriers set up by customs and taxes, and masters the oceans. Christ's commission to the Church to preach the gospel throughout the world today encounters very different obstacles from those of the past. The problems of the missions have become fundamental Christian problems because the very existence of the Church and of Christianity itself is involved. The reaction of the peoples of Asia and Africa against colonialism must be surmounted while the Europeanism of missionary methods needs to be replaced by a well-considered policy of accommodation. A general council offers great possibilities for finding practical solutions and for initiating truly human relations.

Most of the councils were concerned with the removal of schisms, or the re-establishment of unity of belief in a united Church. Everybody can see that after half a century of the ecumenical movement, without the participation of the Catholic Church, the problem of the unity of all Christians is more acute than ever, though whether, and if at all, in what measure, the bishops and the ruling authorities of the Eastern and the reformed Churches could be brought into it, must remain an open question. Canon Law has defined who is entitled to participate at a council of the Church. But it might well be that, on the model of medieval councils and for specific purposes, invitations might be extended to others beyond the determined circle of participants.

It has always been the highest duty of a council to assure the proclamation of the faith by delimiting the Catholic doctrine from contemporary errors. There have been councils which issued no disciplinary canons, but none at which some error was not rejected, or some heretic excluded from the community of the faithful. No error of our time is fraught with greater possibilities of evil than the atheistic doctrines of communism with their caricature of the Christian ideal of human dignity which they actually seek to destroy, and no truth of the faith is in greater need of a clear definition than the concept of the Church.

Church historians are not prophets. They do not presume to offer unsolicited advice to the responsible leaders of the Church. All they are competent to attempt is to deepen our understanding of the present and to offer a glimpse into the future, on the strength of their acquaintance with the past.

BIBLIOGRAPHY

I

This bibliography cannot claim to cover, even in a fragmentary fashion, the vast history of the councils. It is intended in the first place to draw attention to the works of authors which I have used and occasionally quoted in the text. Its further purpose is to acquaint the reader with the means that will enable him to add to the knowledge he may already possess. After a general bibliography there follow more specific ones for each of the five chapters.

For the General History of the Councils

No sectional area of Church history has been supported by the publication of sources at so early a date and on so vast a scale as the history of the councils. Even hagiography is no exception. Only two generations after the invention of the printing press Jacques Merlin's collection, in two volumes, of conciliar acts and decrees, though a very inadequate one, was published in Paris in the year 1525. The Fathers of the Council of Trent had at their disposal an enlarged edition of this work by the Franciscan Peter Crabbe of Malines. The first edition, in two volumes, was published in 1538, the second in three volumes in 1551, by Quentel, a printer of Cologne. The third edition, now grown into four volumes, was published by the Carthusian Lawrence Surius in 1567. A fourth five volume edition was published in 1606 by Severinus Bini, Canon of Cologne.

These first editions of the councils contained only Latin texts. Greek original texts were first printed in the Roman edition of the *Concilia generalia* commissioned by Sixtus V, but which only appeared under Paul V, from 1608 to 1612. It is the only edition of an official character. After that the French took the lead. The Paris edition of 1644, "The Royal Edition," a sumptious one, consisted of thirty-seven volumes in folio, but it was far surpassed, as regards the contents, by the *Sacrosancta Concilia* by two members of the Society of Jesus, Philip Labbé and Gabriel Gossart, which appeared in seventeen volumes, in 1671-2 in Paris. This edition was in its turn surpassed by the *Collectio Regia Maxima* of the Jesuit Jean Hardouin, in twelve volumes, but owing to difficulties with the censorship it was only made available in 1725, fifteen years after it had been printed. It was far better than any previous editions because its author had brought the most exacting criticism to bear on the subject.

After that the leadership passed once more to the Italians. Building on what French scholarship had gathered, Sebastian Coleti published at Venice, between 1728 and 1733, a collection which was a sequel to that of Labbé-Cossart and consisted of thirty-one volumes. Finally John Dominic Mansi published at Florence, between 1759 and 1798, his *Amplissima Collectio*, in thirty-one volumes. Mansi's *Collectio* has remained the standard edition of the sources for a history of the councils. This explains why a revision was undertaken in 1899-1927 by Petit and Martin at Lyons. This edition contains, besides the earlier councils, the general, as well as the more important particular, councils from the sixteenth to the nineteenth century. It is in sixty volumes.

Dom H. Quentin, O.S.B., gives an account of the formation of these earlier collections of the councils in his *I. D. Mansi et les grandes collections conciliaires* (1900).

Modern editions of the sources, based on recent research among manuscripts, exist for the third, fourth and fifth ecumenical councils only, and for those of Constance, Basle-Ferrara-Florence and Trent. These will be mentioned in the different sections that follow.

The most comprehensive presentation of the history of the councils up to the present day is that of C. J. Hefele, subsequently Bishop of Rottenburg, Württemberg. The work, based on Hardouin and Mansi, consists of nine volumes published between 1855 and 1890, (Volumes 8 and 9 are by E. Hergenröther; volumes 1-6 appeared in a second edition). This standard work has been translated into French and brought up to the present state of research by the late Dom H. Leclercq, O.S.B. (*Histoire des Conciles,* 1907-21). Both works go only as far as the fifth Lateran Council. The continuation for the Council of Trent, by P. Richard, appeared in 1930-1. A survey, though by no means complete, of the more recent literature on the history of the councils may be found in my paper: "Nouvelles données sur l'histoire des Conciles" in *Cahiers d'histoire mondiale,* i (1953), pp. 164-78. Articles on the councils in general and short accounts of individual councils are likewise to be found in the great theological encyclopedias. I only mention the *Dictionnaire de théologie catholique* (from 1903); the *Lexikon für Theologie und Kirche* (2nd edition from 1957); and *Die Religion in Geschichte und Gegenwart* (3rd edition from 1957).

The dogmatic definitions of the councils, in the original text, are found in H. Denzinger - J. B. Umberg, *Enchiridion Symbolorum,* 29th edition (1954). For information on the position of the councils in juridical and constitutional history, cf. H. E. Feine, *Kirchliche Rechtsgeschichte,* 2nd edition (1954); P.

Hinschius, *Kirchenrecht,* iii (1883), pp. 325-666, remains a classic.

The most important work on the sources, one that goes beyond Mansi, is the *Acta Conciliorum Oecumenicorum,* edited by Eduard Schwartz, 4 parts, in 25 volumes (1914 to 1940), which includes the sources for the third, fourth and fifth ecumenical councils. Of the many dissertations that accompany Schwartz's great work I mention only the last: E. Schwartz, "Uber die Bischofslisten der Synoden von Chalkedon, Nicaea und Konstantinopel" in *Abhandlungen der Bayr. Akademie der Wiss., Phil. Hist. Klasse,* N. F. (1937), 13. On the convocation and confirmation of the old councils, F. X. Funk has done pioneer's work in his *Kirchengeschichtliche Abhandlungen und Untersuchungen,* i (1897), pp. 39-121. More markedly than Funk, C. A. Kneller has stressed the role of the Popes in the old councils in his "Papst und Konzil im ersten Jahrtausend" in *Zeitschrift für katholische Theologie,* 27 (1903), pp. 1-36, 391-428, with continuations in the following years. More recently on the same subject, F. Dvornik, "Emperors, Popes and General Councils" in *Dumbarton Oakes Papers,* 6 (1951), pp. 1-23. A short but accurate presentation of the Trinitarian and Christological controversies, in K. Bihlmeyer-H. Tüchle, *Kirchengeschichte,* i, 12th ed. (1951). The canons of the early councils may be seen at a glance in the work of the same title, by G. F. Lambert (1896). The quotations in the text are taken from Kösel's *Bibliothek der Kirchenväter.*

For the Council of Chalcedon, the collective work published by the Jesuits of St. Georgen, Frankfort: A. Grillmaier-H.Bacht, *Das Konzil von Chalkedon, Geschichte und Gegenwart,* 3 vols. (1951-4). For information on political and social conditions, especially at the time of the old councils, G. Ostrogorsky's

Geschichte des Byzantinischen Staates, 2nd ed. (1952) is indispensable. The passages on the seventh ecumenical council from Theophanes' "Chronicle of the world," are quoted after L. Breyer, *Bilderstreit und Arabertum in Byzanz* (1957). For Photius: F. Dvornik, *Le schisme de Photios. Histoire et légende* (1950).

II

The sources are to be found mainly in Mansi and Raynald's *Kirchengeschichtliche Annalen.* Besides Hefele and Leclercq, the histories of the Popes should also be consulted: sober and reliable, F. X. Seppelt, *Geschichte der Päpste,* ii-iv (1955-7): lively but at times one-sided in its judgments, *Das Papsttum,* iii-v (1952-3), by J. Haller.

For an understanding of the transition from antiquity to the Middle Ages, A Hauck, "Die Rezeption und Umbildung der allgemeinen Synode im Mittelalter" in *Historische Vierteljahrschrift,* 10 (1907), pp. 465-82 remains of capital importance. For the data on the participants of the medieval Lateran Councils I have followed G. Tangl, *Die Teilnehmer an den Allgemeinen Konzilien des Mittelalters* (1922); for the fourth Lateran Council I also used H. Tillmann, *Papst Innocenz III* (1954).

Extremely important for the relation of the Popes to the Councils of Lyons are the researches of St. Kuttner, "Die Konstitutionen des ersten Allgemeinen Konzils von Lyon" in *Studia et documenta Historiae et Juris,* 6 (1940), pp. 71-110; "Conciliar Law in the making. The Lyonese Constitutions (1274) of Gregory X in a manuscript at Washington" in *Miscellanea Pio Paschini II* (1949), pp. 39-81. Of capital importance for the Council of Vienne is the monograph of E. Müller, *Das Konzil von Vienne* (1934), which stems from the school of H. Finke.

III

In his *Foundations of Conciliar Theory* (1955), B. Tierney has uncovered the roots of conciliar theory in the schools of Canon Law. For its role in the termination of the Great Schism, F. Blitzenrieder's solid study *Das Generalkonzil im grossen Abendländischen Schisma* (1904) retains its importance. To it must be added: H. Heimpel, *Dietrich von Niem* (1932); V. Martin, *Les origines du Gallicanisme*, 2 vols. (1939); E. F. Jacob, *Studies in the Conciliar Epoch* (1943).

Sources for the Council of Pisa of 1409: J. Vincke, "Acta Concilii Pisani" in *Römische Quartalschrift*, 46 (1938), pp. 81-331, as well as *Briefe zum Pisaner Konzil* (1940) by the same author, and *Schriftstücke zum Pisaner Konzil* (1942). The account of the negotiations with Benedict XIII is taken from F. Ehrle, *Martin von Alpartils Cronica actitatorum temporibus Benedicti XIII* (1906).

In addition to the colorful chronicle of Ulrich von Richental, of M. R. Buck (edn. 1882), information on the Council of Constance is found in the great collections of sources by H. Finke, H. Heimpel and J. Hollnsteiner, *Acta Concilii Constantiensis*, 4 vols. (1896-1928); also H. Finke, *Bilder vom Konstanzer Konzil* (1903); the best summary description, J. Hollnsteiner, *Die Kirche im Ringen um die christliche Gemeinschaft* (1940), pp. 269-94.

The most important work on the Council of Basle, based on the sources, is *Concilium Basiliense*, ed. J. Haller, H. Herre and G. Beckmann, 8 vols. (1896-1936). A similar work for Ferrara-Florence is *Concilium Florentinum*, published by the Papal Oriental Institute in Rome, 6 vols. (1940-55), and the dissertation by the principal editor G. Hofmann, *Papato, Conciliarismo, Patriarcato* (1959). The most recent work on the Council of Florence: Joseph Gill, S.J.,

The Council of Florence (Cambridge University Press, 1959).

In the first volume of my *History of the Council of Trent* (Nelson, Edinburgh, 1957) I give a survey of the after-effects of conciliar theory in the fifteenth century and at the beginning of the sixteenth.

IV

The decrees of the Council of Trent were printed in 1564 by Paul Manutius in an official edition and since then they have been reprinted over and over again. St. Kuttner has published a facsimile edition of Massarelli's autograph protocol of the first nine sessions with an excellent introduction: *Decreta septem priorum sessionum Concilii Tridentini sub Paulo III* (1945). A Michel, *Les décrets du Concile de Trente* (1938) gives a brief account of their formation. *Concilium Tridentinum,* published by the Görres-Gesellschaft, though still incomplete, is the most authoritative work on the sources. So far twelve volumes have appeared (1901-50), in four parts, containing diaries, protocols, letters and tractates. The story of the study of the Council of Trent, an exciting story in fact, is described in my book, *Das Konzil von Trient. Ein Uberblick über die Erforschung seiner Geschichte* (1948). The immediate preliminaries of the council and its first period are described in my *History of the Council of Trent.* For its last period my book *Krisis und Wendepunkt des Trienter Konzils* (1941) should also be consulted. I have contributed a survey of the centenary literature before and after 1945 to the compilation published by G. Schreiber, *Das Weltkonzil von Trient,* i (1950), pp. 11-31. H. Jedin, "Rede und Stimmfreiheit auf dem Konzil von Trient" in *Historisches Jahrbuch,* 75 (1956), pp. 73-93. For the printed lists of participants, see G. Alberigo, "Cataloghi dei partecipanti al Concilio di

Trento editi durante il medesimo" in *Rivista di storia della Chiesa in Italia,* 10 (1956), pp. 345-73; 11 (1957), pp. 49-94; the same: *I vescovi Italiani al Concilio di Trento* (1958). C. Guttiérrez, *Españoles en Trento* (1951). For the execution of the decrees, L. Pastor, *History of the Popes,* xii-xvi (London, 1950). A report on their execution in Italy by G. Alberigo, "Studi e problemi relativi all'applicazione dello Concilio di Trento in Italia" in *Rivista storica Italiana,* 70 (1958), pp. 239-98.

V

The protocols of the Vatican Council are to be found in Petit's continuation of Mansi's *Amplissima Collectio,* vol. 49-53 (1923-7). Side by side with it the *Collectio Lacensis,* vii (1892), published by the Jesuits Schneemann and Granderath, should also be consulted because it contains many texts not found in Mansi. The best general description is that of Th. Granderath, *Geschichte des Vatikanischen Konzils,* 3 vols. (1903-6). *The Vatican Council, The Story from inside told in Bishop Ullathorne's letters* (Longmans, 1930) has served me as an invaluable source for quotations. Shorter accounts: J. Schmidlin, *Papstgeschichte der neuesten Zeit,* ii (1934), pp. 255-92; the best is R. Aubert, *Le pontificat de Pie IX* (1952), pp. 311-67; also by the same, "Documents concernant le tiers parti au Concile du Vatican" in *Festschrift Karl Adam* (1952), pp. 241-59.

*　　*　　*

English readers will find short authoritative accounts of all the councils in *The Catholic Encyclopedia.* The medieval councils and their circumstances are described in Msgr. H. Maur's *Lives of the Popes in the Middle Ages;* those of the fifteenth and sixteenth centuries in L. Pastor, *History of the Popes* (London, 1950).

CHRONOLOGICAL TABLE

1 First Council of Nicaea, May 20 to July 25 [?], 325. Pope Sylvester I, 314-35. Nicene Creed against Arius: the Son consubstantial with the Father. Twenty canons. Page 20.

2 First Council of Constantinople, May to July, 381. Pope Damasus I, 366-84. Nicene-Constantinopolitan Creed: the divinity of the Holy Ghost. Four canons. Page 26.

3 Council of Ephesus: five sessions, June 22 to July 17, 431. Pope Celestine I, 422-32. Mary, the Mother of God against Nestorius. Six canons. Page 32.

4 Council of Chalcedon. Seventeen sessions, October 8 to November 1, 451. Pope Leo I, the Great, 440-61. Two natures in the one person of Christ. Twenty-eight canons. Page 37.

5 Second Council of Constantinople. Eight sessions, May 5 to June 2, 553. Pope Vigilius, 537-55. Condemnation of the "Three Chapters" of the Nestorians. Page 39.

6 Third Council of Constantinople. Sixteen sessions, November 7, 680, to September 16, 681 (in Trullo). Pope Agatho, 678-81; Pope Leo II, 662-

3. Condemnations of the doctrine of one will in Christ (Monotheletism); Question of Honorius. Page 42.

7 Second Council of Nicaea. Eight sessions, September 24 to October 23, 787. Pope Hadrian I, 772-95. Meaning and lawfulness of the veneration of images. Twenty canons. Page 45.

8 Fourth Council of Constantinople. Ten sessions, October 5 to February 28, 870. Pope Nicholas I, 858-67; Hadrian II, 867-72. Termination of the schism of Patriarch Photius. Twenty-seven canons. Page 49.

9 First Lateran Council, March 18 to April 6, 1123. Pope Callistus II, 1119-24. Confirmation of the Concordat of Worms. Twenty-five canons. Page 57.

10 Second Lateran Council, April, 1139. Pope Innocent II, 1130-43. Schism of Anacletus II. Thirty canons. Page 59.

11 Third Lateran Council. Three sessions, March 5 to 19 (or 22), 1179. Pope Alexander III, 1159-81. Twenty-seven chapters; two-thirds majority for papal election. Page 61.

12 Fourth Lateran Council. Three sessions, November 11 to 30, 1215. Pope Innocent III, 1198-1216. Seventy chapters: Profession of faith against the Cathari; change of substance in the Eucharist; annual confession and Communion. Page 64.

13 First Council of Lyons. Three sessions, June 28 to July 17, 1245. Pope Innocent IV, 1243-54. Deposition of the Emperor Frederick II. Twenty-two chapters. Page 68.

14 Second Council of Lyons. Six sessions, May 7 to July 17, 1274. Pope Gregory X, 1271-76. Rules for conclave, union with the Greeks, crusade. Thirty-one chapters. Page 71.

15 Council of Vienne. Three sessions, October 16, 1311, to May 6, 1312. Pope Clement V, 1305-14. Suppression of the Order of the Templars. Controversy over Franciscan poverty. Reform decrees. Page 78.

16 Council of Constance. Forty-five sessions, November 5, 1414, to April 22, 1418. Termination of the Great Schism; resignation of the Roman Pope Gregory XII (1405-15), on July 4, 1415; deposition of the conciliar Pope John XXIII (1410-15) on May 29, 1415; deposition of the Avignon Pope, Benedict XIII (1394-1415) on July 26, 1417. Election of Martin V, November 11, 1417. Condemnation of John Hus. Decree *Sacrosancta* on the superiority of the Council over the Pope and decree *Frequens* on the periodicity of the councils. Concordats with five conciliar nations. Page 89.

17 Council of Basle-Ferrara-Florence. At Basle twenty-five sessions, July 23, 1431, to May 7, 1437. Translation to Ferrara by Eugenius IV (1431-47) on September 18, 1437, finally on January 1, 1438; from there to Florence, January 16, 1439. Union with the Greeks, July 6, 1439, with the Armenians, November 22, 1439, with the Jacobites, February 4, 1442. Translation to Rome, April 25, 1442. Page 100.

18 Fifth Lateran Council. Twelve sessions, May 10, 1512, to March 16, 1517. Pope Julius II, 1503-13; Leo X, 1513-21. Against the schismatic Council of Pisa, 1511 to 12, Reform decrees. Page 108.

19 Council of Trent. Twenty-five sessions, December 13, 1545, to December 4, 1563, in three periods: sessions 1-8 at Trent, 1545-47; sessions 9-11, at Bologna, 1547, all under Paul III, 1534-49; sessions 12-16 again at Trent, 1551-52, under Pope Julius III, 1550-55, sessions 17-25 at Trent under Pius IV, 1559-65. Doctrine of Scripture and Tradition, Original sin and justification, sacraments and Sacrifice of the Mass, veneration of the Saints, reform decrees. Page 111.

20 Council of the Vatican. Four sessions, December 8, 1869, to July 18, 1870. Pope Pius IX, 1846-78. Definitions of Catholic doctrine, the Pope's primacy and his infallibility. Page 143.